CAROLE TOWNSEND

RED LIPSTICK AND CLEAN UNDERWEAR

Carole Townsend is a former marketing executive, wife and mother living in the suburbs of Atlanta Georgia. Since she was a young girl, she always dreamed of writing stories and books that mirror real life, yet still make readers laugh. Putting that dream on hold to focus on her career and family, she finally decided that it was her time to explore her love of writing when her youngest child left for college. Becoming a newspaper reporter nearly ten years ago fueled that desire, and she published her first book, *Southern Fried White Trash,* in 2011. Her eclectic wit and right-on perspective became her trademark.

BOOKS BY CAROLE TOWNSEND

Southern Fried White Trash

Red Lipstick and Clean Underwear

RED LIPSTICK
AND
CLEAN UNDERWEAR

To Norma,
Enjoy!
Carol Alexander

RED LIPSTICK
AND
CLEAN UNDERWEAR

CAROLE TOWNSEND

CRABGRASS PUBLISHING, LLC.

Edited By: Michelle Couch

Crabgrass Publishing, LLC
PO Box 490640
Lawrenceville, Ga. 30049

wwww.crabgrasspublishing.com

DEDICATION

Dedicated, with my sincerest thanks, to women, especially those who took the time to share their stories with me so that I may share them with others.

A special thank-you to Marc, who always pushes me to believe in myself.

Thank you to Gabrielle and Natalie, who were such good sports about stepping back into time to pose for the cover of this book. You're beautiful, ladies.

Sincere thanks and special recognition to Stan of "Stan's Salon" for welcoming our photo-shoot crew to his 40-year-old beauty shop in Athens, GA. The roots of this beauty shop have a little touch of Hollywood to them, as the vintage-style dryer chairs were actually used on the movie set of "Steel Magnolias." Robert, thanks for telling me about this treasure located right here in Georgia.

Thanks to Michelle, for lending her professional eyes and ears. What would I do without you?

And thank-you to the Vaughan family, for kindly allowing me to use their lovely writer's hideaway at the beach.

It really does take a village to raise a book.

"The great question that has never been answered, and which I have not yet been able to answer, despite my thirty years of research into the feminine soul, is,
'What does a woman want?'"
– Sigmund Freud

"The woman I was yesterday, introduced me to the woman I am today, which makes me very excited about meeting the woman I will become tomorrow."
— Poetic Evolution

TABLE OF CONTENTS

CAN WE TALK?

Before we get started, I want to offer a deeply sincere thank-you to all the women who took the time to sit down with me and share their life experiences, both the new friends and the not-so-new ones. I've met women whose personal accounts have touched my own life, and I am so very grateful for their frankness and honesty in sharing what I've come to affectionately call "Mama's advice." What a delight to share openly the mysterious potion that we women brew, drink and serve to others throughout our lifetimes. The research involved in writing this book has benefitted me more than I could have ever imagined; women from all over the country, from all walks of life, eagerly shared both their mothers' advice as well as their own hard-earned truths.

I've had many people ask me whether this book is about Southern women, and I suppose that's a fair enough question, considering the fact that I'm a Southern writer (and a woman, at that). I'll take it one step further and say that in my mind, the book did begin with a Southern spin and humorous highlight. The South and all that it inspires are, after all, my comfort zone. However, after interviewing so many women of diverse backgrounds over the past year during my research, it became obvious that the direction of the book needed to change. I came to realize that the stories told, advice bestowed and affairs-of-the-heart shared, from one generation of women to the next, are absolutely and uniquely universal. Oh, perhaps the words varied from region to region, but the sentiments and rock-solid truths remained exactly the same.

Something else I learned is that it takes great courage for a woman to speak openly about many of the things she experiences in her life. In truth, what I originally intended to be a humorous book about the inconsistencies between Mama's advice and what it actually takes to get through life has evolved into something much bigger, more complex and far more reverent (though I do hope you chuckle aloud a few times as you're reading).

As an aside, one of my girlfriends asked me whether I drew any of my ideas for this book from what are widely considered the consummate female classic movies: "Steel Magnolias" and "Fried Green Tomatoes." When I hung my head and confessed that I had never seen "Steel Magnolias", she was shocked to say the least. I explained that because I am an Olympic crier, I avoid watching movies that could possibly invoke an occurrence of epic waterworks. Once they start, I simply cannot stop them. I do know women who watch emotionally charged movies for the express purpose of crying their eyes out. They explain the experience to be cleansing and cathartic for the soul; however I can out-cry anyone in the room, and it does not make me feel good in any way afterward. For me, it is embarrassing, because I literally cannot control it. I feel badly afterward, find myself dealing with retaliatory sinuses, and it just makes me look "puffy." And ladies, you know what I mean by "puffy."

Anyway, I actually felt kind of bad, inept really, when my friend reacted the way she did when I said I'd never seen "Steel Magnolias," so within a week of our conversation, I womaned up and watched it. Fabulous movie; great actresses. I cried like a baby, my eyes puffed up and stayed swollen for two whole days, and I sounded like I had a cold when I spoke but I will say this: the words and events and situations in the movie rang true. They rang straight and solid and true, hitting home with probably millions of women over the years. Now I can honestly say that I understand why women rave about that film. If you haven't seen it, you should, but grab a couple of boxes of tissues first. I'm warning you.

If you were born by the mid-sixties, give or take a little, and otherwise known as a member of the baby boomer generation, then I'm guessing that you know exactly what this book's title, "Red Lipstick and Clean Underwear," refers to. Our female, pre-"generation-X" demographic has seen and lived many changes over the years. I'd say we've brought more than a few of them about. I think we can also say that we've had to learn to think on our feet, to simultaneously be flexible, unbending, open-minded and hard-headed in order to survive and to build good lives. Fortunately, women are genetically pre-wired to do all that and more. But every generation of us has had to be all these things and a bag of chips to simply endure, so why write a book about it?

As a young woman growing up in suburban Atlanta, I recall as though it were yesterday, hearing mothers tell their daughters that they'd need a few critical things to get through life: girlhood, pre-teens, single adulthood, marriage and finally fulfilled wife-and-motherhood. Were these truly our ultimate destinations on the merry-go-round of womanhood? Or were they simply an array of programmed responses passed down from one generation of women to the next?

Here in the South, we put our own particular spin on what makes a woman a real woman. You'll never hear me say that we in the South are backward (quite the opposite, if you understand us at all), but the "old South" (which is still very much alive, though its stately population is dwindling) draws a hard line. A woman is expected to be proper, well educated, beautiful, charitable, the ideal hostess, a perfect homemaker and impeccably dressed at all times, following the old Southern rule book. Incidentally, these rules aren't written down anywhere in a single easy-reference manual; they're unspoken and taught by example from one generation of women to the next. Yes, the Vanderbilts and the Posts collected and published etiquette tomes jam-packed with rules -- Behavioral Bibles to many through the years -- but even so, there are many more teachings that are undocumented, quietly passed on from woman to woman. These secret rules are also the reason for many a secret drinking habit and nervous breakdown, in my opinion, but it is what it is.

I admittedly fall woefully short of the old South's standards for what constitutes a proper woman, but I'm O.K. with that. With the bustling diversity that characterizes Atlanta and her sister cities here in the South, women are using a wider brush and more vivid colors to paint their lives, thank sweet

Heaven. The freedom feels much like taking off a girdle after wearing it all day long (or so I've been told).

In my case, my mother did expect me to go to college, and she very much encouraged it, but I think she was secretly holding out hope that college would help bolster my stellar secretarial skills (of which I had none) and maybe help me corral a suitable husband to boot. Had she lived to see me graduate college, she would have been sorely disappointed on both fronts.

At any rate, thanks to the important women I had in my life as a young woman, I grew up believing that no matter what, a fresh coat of lipstick (and with time, other makeup to boot) applied just before walking out the door would make any errand or adventure infinitely better, more promising. "Who knows who you might run into?" was the logic behind the theory. These women practiced what they preached, too. Even a simple stroll to the mailbox involved a full-on facial involving Mary Kay, Avon, Elizabeth Arden, Merle Norman or whatever a Southern lady's personal poison may have been.

I remember as a child, sneaking into my parents' bedroom just to play with my mother's makeup and admire the tempting bottles of perfume she kept on a mirrored tray on her dresser. Tabu and Chanel No. 5 were her favorite scents, and I thought the bottles were just so beautiful. I didn't dare open them or spray any of the secret, alluring liquid on myself; otherwise, there would never be any denying that I had been tampering in her beauty arsenal. Funny the things you remember from childhood, isn't it? Funny too that to this day, I can't stand the smell of either of those scents. Freud would probably have a few things to say about that.

Do you remember hearing this one when you were rushing to get out the door: "Whatever you do, be sure you have on clean underwear, and Heaven forbid there be any holes in it!" The reason for this time-worn pearl of wisdom, of course, was that should there be the awful misfortune of a serious accident, paramedics and rubber-necking bystanders would be treated to the sight of undies which are perfectly presentable and in good working order. Of course, Mama assured us that clean underwear ultimately guarantees the best possible triage and trauma care.

When my daughters asked me about the universally famous underwear adage, they laughed in disbelief when I explained it. "What does your underwear have to do with having a car accident?" they asked, and all I could muster was, "I don't know. It just does." In truth, it was an appearance thing, as in, "What on earth would people think if they saw you splayed out all over the road with holes in your underwear?" Those were the kinds of things that mattered to our elders, I suppose. Oh, if only my mother had an inkling about what my underwear looked like on so many occasions when I left the house, even today. She'd have been mortified.

Our mothers meant well. They were pulling from the wisdom of their mothers who, of course, in turn relied on their mothers for a roadmap to navigating the life of being a woman. Born in 1925, my own mother was one of nine children raised on a Virginia farm. She was different from her sisters; she often said that she had always aspired to be more than a farmer's wife, which of course was the destiny of most women with whom she grew up. She was cut out for different things, that's for sure. She was undeniably ahead of her time, especially for her generation. In fact, she was almost too business-like to be considered lady-like; at least that's how many people saw her back in the '50s and '60s. I remember when I was a child, and my mother would take time out of her busy workday to attend a parent-teacher conference at my school; the look of surprise and even disapproval on the other mothers' faces was always evident. I doubt that my mother ever paid enough attention to notice the looks, nor would she have cared. But I know that, for some reason, I did.

I've often wondered how far she would have climbed up the corporate ladder had she been born 50 or so years later than she was. She may very well have owned the thing. But like so many women in the workforce during that time period, the powers-that-be didn't even bother making the ceiling out of glass; it was very definitely thick, reinforced concrete, and no one made any apologies for it.

As a girl growing up in the '60s and '70s in suburban Atlanta, most of my friends' moms were either "stay-at-home" moms, or they worked part-time jobs to bring in some extra money. Many families were still one-car families, so often moms would provide childcare to the two-parent working families in order to earn extra income (daycare centers had yet to appear on the scene, revolutionizing the work force and opening all kinds of doors for women, for better or for worse). My mother was the exception in my circle of friends; she worked a full-time job, commuting back and forth from the city to the suburbs each day, blazing a trail for millions of women to follow in later years. It was not easy, but my mother was not the stay-at-home type. In hindsight, that was most definitely for the best. Some women are actually better mothers if they earn a living outside the home, don't you agree? They need what a career gives them; they just desire "more," however they define that added fulfillment.

Still, Mom passed down the lipstick-and-underwear wisdom to me, because that's the advice she must have been given from someone she must have admired, although I doubt it was her mother, since farm wives rarely had time for such nonsense. Tragically, my mother died when I was just 17 years old, so I've clung to the precious little advice I received from her. I have also relied on the advice of many other extraordinary women to help me illustrate and communicate this idea of handed-down knowledge and wives' tales that may or may not apply in the year 2012.

I have to admit that, ever since my mother died in 1978, I've felt a bit short-changed, maybe even a little sorry for myself. I'll also admit (shamefully) that I've sometimes envied other women who still have their mothers. I've wished many times that my mother was still around to know my children, to love them and to spoil them. I was reminded though, while interviewing women for this book, that many girls never really knew their own moms or worse yet, some mothers never take the time to pass on life lessons to their daughters. Some women I have talked to have never even heard the funny tidbits of wisdom from their mamas (those we often refer to as old wives' tales), like "Don't cross your eyes; they'll get stuck like that!" or "Don't crack your knuckles. They'll be huge!" In my opinion, it would be worse to have a mom who didn't put in the time and effort than to have lost one at an early age who would have.

Red lipstick and clean underwear were just two of the many clever clues in a woman's "how to be a woman" toolbox. I've come to the conclusion that much of the advice passed from one generation of women to the next had to do with either proper grooming or with catching a husband. In our moms' generation, life required impeccable grooming and husband-catching skills, yes, but life was also changing for women. Opportunities were opening up to us;

education was becoming an option for which women hungry for options clamored. For the first time, women could consider and choose careers, not just jobs. But the availability of education meant much more for women – and the entire world – than simply opening more lucrative and satisfying career doors. I think the late Brigham Young, an American leader in the Latter Day Saint movement, said it best:

"You educate a man; you educate a man. You educate a woman; you educate a generation."

In this past generation, and in current and future generations, more (not all) women have been introduced to the fact that there are other goals in life besides just marrying and having babies. It must have been exciting; it must have been confusing. It must have been utterly terrifying.

My mother was balancing on a high wire like other women of her generation – teetering on the thin, fine line dividing the past and the future, trying to find a balance between the way life used to be and the way it was becoming.

We, my friends, are living it.

--Carole

Can We Talk

BEING A WOMAN

"Women are in league with each other, a secret conspiracy of hearts and pheromones."
— Camille Paglia
(American author, teacher and social critic)

Let me say right out of the gate that this book is the love-child of three parents: my love of being a woman, my sometimes angst at the same condition, and my weird and off-beat knack for finding humor in pretty much anything. Let me also go on record at the outset to say that this is not a book about man-hating or man-bashing; I love men. Where would we be without them? Rather, this book is an assessment and an examination, a sincere gesture of admiration and a heartfelt tribute to the age-old sisterhood known as "women." This book is a celebration of women and all that we represent – to each other, to our lovers, to our children and to our friends. I wrote this book to take an honest and in-depth look at the complexities of being female –– the good, the bad and the ugly (but in the end, mostly the good and certainly all the beauty).

We women have been referred to through the generations as being many things: nurturers, the weaker sex, broads, God's second shot at getting it right (I didn't coin that one), and the list goes on. The truth of the matter is that we are complex creatures, many things to many people, constantly shape-shifting and mood swinging. We are driven, determined, infuriating, endearing, passionate, persevering, frustrating and fascinating all at once. We are all of these things because, at one time or another in our lives, we have had to be. We are daughters, wives and mothers. We are women.

A very wise marriage and family counselor (a man, mind you) once told me that a woman's life is akin to an intricate, rich tapestry, each event and passage forever woven and connected to all the other events in her life by common threads. He went on to say that a man's life is a series of pigeon holes, each event its own, distinct occurrence and separate from all others in his life. This phenomenon explains, of course, the fact that a couple can have an earth-shattering argument in the afternoon and have very different ideas about whether to make love that same evening. He's on board, sitting on GO. She's busy at the loom, adding to her tapestry. This same counselor told me that, where the rubber meets the road, men are ultimately motivated by two things and two things alone: food and sex. Yes, hopefully money figures into the equation at some point in his life, but an abundance of money simply means more food and more sex, and maybe a nice house or two in which to enjoy both. This observation is not intended to denigrate men; rather, it's just further proof of the age-old theory that men are hunters and conquerors, and women are gatherers and nurturers.

I ran across this humorous presentation of "Women's English" vs. "Men's English" in my research that pretty obviously illustrates the point I'm making about some fundamental differences in the sexes. I can't take credit for these translations, and they can appear rather blunt and crude if taken literally, but hats off to whomever created them. They often prove to be true on some level. Even the pastor of my church has alluded to the concept, though he of course would never use such language:

Women's English

1. Yes = No
2. No = Yes
3. Maybe = No
4. "It's your decision" = The correct decision should be obvious by now.
5. "Do what you want" = You'll pay for this later.
6. "We need to talk" = I need to talk.
7. "Sure, go ahead" = I don't want you to.
8. "I'm not upset" = Of course I'm upset; are you blind?
9. "How much do you love me?" = I did something today, and you're not going to like it.
10. "Is my rear-end fat?" = Tell me I'm beautiful.
11. "You have to learn to communicate." = You have to learn to agree with me.
12. "Are you listening to me?" = Too late, you're dead.

Men's English

1. "I'm hungry" = I'm hungry.
2. "I'm sleepy" = I'm sleepy.
3. "I'm tired" = I'm tired.
4. "Do you want to go to a movie?" = I'd eventually like to have sex with you.
5. "Can I take you to dinner?" = I'd eventually like to have sex with you.
6. Can I call you sometime? = I'd eventually like to have sex with you.
7. "May I have this dance?" = I'd eventually like to have sex with you.
8. "You look tense. Let me give you a massage" = Uh huh. OK.
9. "What's wrong?" = I guess sex tonight is out of the question.
10. "I'm bored" = Do you want to have sex?
11. "I love you" = Let's have sex right now.
12. "I love you too" = Okay I said it. Can we have sex now?
13. "Let's talk" = I am trying to impress you by showing that I'm a deep person, and maybe then you'd like to have sex with me.
14. "Will you marry me?" = I want to make it illegal for you to have sex with other guys.

Of course, this illustration simplifies some very complicated concepts but still, we get why it's funny. Men and women are very different, to say the least, and thank goodness for that. Can you imagine dating and eventually marrying someone who behaved like a woman, especially if you're a woman yourself? I'd be miserable. I don't know why I do some of the things I do half the time; can you imagine being a man, thinking in very concrete terms, and trying to figure out women? No, thank you.

Once my own daughters came of age and I felt that I could address the topic of boys' motives vs. girls' responsibly with them, I tried to save each of them years of frustration and confusion with one brilliantly simple piece of advice. As mothers, we actually believe that we can discover and relate some stroke of genius that our moms overlooked when it comes to having the difficult conversations. For this illustration, I'm talking about one of the many "birds and bees" talks through which I stammered, sweated and blushed. "Don't over-complicate men," I would sagely share with them. Simple enough, right? Oh, how I wish someone had told me that when I was younger. I doubt that I would have had the maturity to really appreciate it, but it's fabulous advice, because it's the truth. It's what we do. When we are in a relationship with a man, we ask ourselves (and him) questions like, "What are you thinking? How do you feel about this or about that?" The answer, if everyone will be brutally honest for a moment, is often "nothing." When you think he's brewing or stewing over an issue, he's really thinking about what's for dinner or whether you're in the mood. Or he's thinking about whether his new female colleague is in the mood. Or he may be wondering whether the checkout girl at the supermarket is in the mood. Or it's quite possible he's thinking about work, or nothing at all. I don't mean to imply that men are stupid or shallow, and I certainly don't mean to insinuate that all men are cads; they're simply wired differently. If you don't believe me, marry one. Again, they are hunters, and we are gatherers. Hunters strategize and act, and gatherers feel and nurture. There. Hopefully I've saved a few of you thousands of dollars in therapy.

"Show up naked and bring food" is the best darned advice a woman can heed with respect to her relationship with a man, said this counselor in his tongue-in-cheek manner. And if only we were wired to think and act in such basic, primitive terms, a woman's life would be oh-so-much simpler, wouldn't it?

Women constantly vacillate between love and hate in their relationships with both food and sex (and with men too, I suppose). And that's why we have this sizzling, popping, zig-zagging fascination with one another, we opposite-sexers. Perhaps one day I'll write a book examining how men are groomed and guided toward being who and how they are, but then again, what do I know on that subject? I suspect it would be a very short book, anyway. I've raised one son and one daughter, helped with two step-daughters, and the experiences were very, very different. For our purposes here, let's stick to women.

From the time we baby boomers were little girls, babies even, so many of us were told that we were pretty and sweet - or that we should be. We were decorated with frilly dresses, ruffled socks and shiny shoes. We were given baby dolls to nurture, play kitchens in which to play cook, play vacuum cleaners and ironing boards (I still haven't figured out what those were for), and pink and shiny trinkets. We were admonished to be peacemakers, not aggressors. These lessons and the props may be changing somewhat as the decades come and go, but I think we can still say that very often, the same parent/child model holds true.

I'll just throw it out there right now that here in the South, it's still the way things work. I know this claim opens up the "nature *vs.* nurture" can of worms, and I promise we'll take a look at that later on. It can't be ignored if we're to take an honest look at either sex, but for our purposes here, again we're assessing women. We Southerners just tend to hold on to "the way things were" a little longer than other people do. It's part of our white-knuckled charm.

Toward the same goal of teaching young, impressionable Southern girls how to grow into happy, adult robo-women, our mothers, grandmothers, and aunts had an adage and lesson for almost any occasion, proffered words of wisdom for their young charges -- if you will, "my dah-lin'."

Now I'm talking to women, say, age 35 and better when I make this claim. There are too many maxims to list here, but in doing some of my research, I've talked with dozens of women, asking them what pearls of wisdom their elders handed down to them when they were younger. Here are just a few, to give you an idea of where I'm going with this:

Never leave the house without makeup, or at least a fresh coat of lipstick. You never know when you'll meet Mr. Right.

Never leave the house with holey, or God forbid, dirty underwear on. What if you get into a car accident?

Always keep a dime in your shoe, in case you need to make a phone call (nowadays, kids can keep the whole phone in their shoe).

You can always tell a lady by what the inside of her purse looks like (Lord help me).

Whenever you feel down, vacuum. It'll make you feel better.

Nice Women don't smoke (Audrey Hepburn in
"Breakfast at Tiffany's" made us re-think
that one).

Nice women don't smoke in public
(confusing, I know).

Nice girls don't eat in public
(Boy have I blown it on that one).

Be sure to learn typing (and yes, for some of us,
shorthand) to get you by just until you marry. After
that, your husband will take care of you.

A girl lets a boy chase her until she's caught him.

Familiarity breeds contempt, AND Absence makes
the heart grow fonder (figure those two out).

Do not use men to buy you stuff. If you do, call it
what it is and don't sugar-coat it. It's prostitution.

Your life won't start until you meet your husband.

You will catch more flies with honey than you will
with vinegar.

Be modest; why have all your goods unwrapped,
leaving nothing for the imagination?

The dog that brings a bone will carry a bone (referring to gossip – love that one).

Always wear earrings so you won't catch a cold (my friend Marilyn swears by this one).

Never tell your husband "no."

Always have dinner on the table at 5:00.

Don't let the last thing your husband sees as he's leaving for work be you, in a bathrobe and curlers.

Never have children in an attempt to fill a void, make you happy or fix a relationship. A child can do none of those things and should not be expected to.

If you're going to attend any event, be sure you're the best-dressed woman there, or don't go at all.

And from Julia, whom I met on the beach in the dead of winter while writing this book,

"Always eat the crusts of your bread. They'll make you pretty." Never heard that one, but I love it. I've since heard several other women back it up.

You likely see a repeating theme here, as did I. The bulk of the advice coming from our moms had to do with grooming, appearances and bagging a man -- catching one, landing one, whichever term you prefer to use. Precious little of their advice addressed what to do once you had him though, did it? Their advice rarely told us how to steer through or around true heartbreak, no matter how hard or fast it came at us. The whole phenomenon of incomplete advice reminds me of those priceless "What to Expect When You're Expecting" books. They were great, weren't they? But where was the book that outlined what to do with the baby once he or she arrived? Now that one would have been a sure-fire bestseller in my day. In fact, I think that someone finally wrote that very book and it is, in fact, a bestseller. What a lifesaver, provided you have time to sit down and read it once the baby arrives.

The list of proverbs and advice from Mama goes on and on. Our moms had the best of intentions, and I don't think anyone will deny that what we learn about being women we learn primarily from our mothers, oh and sometimes from Cosmo Magazine.

The mother/daughter relationship is fascinating to me. Our daughters start out as innocent, trusting babies just the same as our sons do; Mommy is their world, and Daddy, an easy mark. But then something happens in the adolescent and teen years; it seems that mothers and daughters come dangerously close to the brink of becoming enemies, or at the very least becoming somewhat estranged from each other. It used to sadden and even frighten me, the level of animosity that it sometimes seemed my girls had toward me during these years. If I'd say "black," they would say "white." If I said "up," they'd answer (through gritted teeth and clenched jaws) with "down." But in between those battles we were close, and I'd revel in every minute of that. My youngest daughter -- precariously close to exhibiting some of her mom's own perplexing traits — would write me letters when she felt frustrated or confined by my parenting. I've saved every one of them; they're priceless to me. She would say things to me in these letters that, if I didn't know her and love her so much, might have been cutting and hurtful. She was, after all, in middle school. The venom constantly drips from their young, ever-exposed fangs during those tumultuous years, doesn't it? To me, it certainly seemed that way. She would vent about what all of her other friends were allowed to do while she had to sit on the sidelines because she had one of "those moms." She would shame me for having the nerve to try to tell her how to dress, how to pick her friends, how to conduct herself in certain situations. Come to think of it, I think I'll laminate those letters. She'll need to refer to them when she has her own girls, and I'll be happy to provide copies of them, in triplicate.

I have since come to understand that this is precisely how a girl sharpens the skills of becoming her own woman; mom is the whetstone; she, the blade. Sparks fly, there's friction and intense heat, but the end result is a more mellow whetstone and a shiny, razor-sharp knife. We do become the best of friends with our daughters further down the road in life, so to any of you who are struggling through the adolescent/teen phase right now, hang in there.

One of the methods with which our moms taught us was using the wise (and sometimes profoundly silly) sayings we've inherited from the generations before us. Some hardly apply any longer, but who could have foreseen the changes that, at least back then, were only tiny specks, social and lifestyle dust-ups on the horizon of a woman's world? Yet the harbingers were there, and today they have mushroomed into life circumstances that include single motherhood, challenging careers, divorce, blended families, caring for elderly parents, and even health issues that we're now living long enough to look in the eye and hopefully be the last to blink.

Somehow, red lipstick and clean underwear don't seem to matter so much anymore, do they?.

THE EARLY YEARS

*"The best way to learn to be a lady is to see
how other ladies do it."*
– Mae West
(American actress, playwright and screenwriter)

Statistically speaking, there are estimated to be about 107 boys born to every 100 girls each year, globally. I should be mindful here and note that this is a Central Intelligence Agency estimate, found in the CIA Fact Book, according to Wikipedia. It was probably deduced by a group of men and a computer program, so take it for what it's worth. Men tend to be somewhat competitive. Let's assume the statistic is accurate; if so, the CIA itself says girls are outnumbered right from the get-go.

In some cultures, female babies are considered expendable, and selective abortion is still routinely practiced. That notion is absolutely inconceivable to me. Nonetheless, it happens even today. There are many reasons given for this barbaric practice, but suffice it to say, baby boys are often placed much higher on the totem pole than are girls. Why?

Well I suppose it goes back to the idea of a stronger *vs.* a weaker sex. Even in our own country and not very long ago, male children were prized over female children simply because of the family's need for strong backs on the farm.

The logical extrapolation of the practice of weeding out little girls in a society is the eventual extinction of that same society, for obvious reasons. In other words, it takes both sexes to tango. Too, I can picture a tribe of men, strategically and skimpily wrapped in leather, sitting around a slain deer or wild hog wondering who in the heck is going to cook it. They'd starve to death, if nothing else.

Right from birth, tiny girls are in a fight for survival. When I hear the terrible tales of selective abortion or outright female infanticide, the analogy that comes to my mind is the epic struggle of the tiny sea turtle, who from the moment she claws her way out of that shell is in a fight for her life. If the gulls and lizards and other creatures don't snap her up for an appetizer while she is making a run for her life to the water, the sheer heat of the sun on the sand may fry her in her tracks. Even if she should make it to the water's edge, she's hardly home free, as that's where the real danger lurks. In the end, it's determination, instinct, eventual skill but mostly luck that escort the baby turtles to adulthood. Can't the same be said of the journey from young girl to adult woman, and how well we fare? This is probably a good time to give a nod to the "*nature vs. nurture*" issue with respect to girls' and boys' behavior, as I promised we'd do at some point. I'm not a scientist, nor do I pretend to be one on TV, but I'll always remember vividly a behavioral research experiment I witnessed years ago that addressed this very subject. I thought the concept of the experiment spoke volumes and that the conclusions were profound. In it, children (some boys, some girls, each examined one at a time) were separated from their mothers by a clear plastic wall. While both sexes soon exhibited anxiety by the imposed separation, the little boys eventually tried to push or kick the wall down to get to Mommy, screaming and pounding in frustration and sometimes even in anger. The little girls cried, tried to verbalize, and pleadingly held their arms out in an attempt to solve the problem that way.

Boys. Girls. Aggression. Verbalization.

Interesting.

Of course, if we were to revisit those same children all grown up say, in their forties, we might see different approaches to the problem. Something deliciously profound happens to women in the fourth decade of their lives, and I suspect we'd probably see some fascinating approaches to the same problem, if in fact she still wanted to get to her mom, and provided she wanted to do so for the right reasons. Anyway, I'm thinking that men would be more desperate to reach their mommies at age forty than they ever were at age two. Dr. Sigmund Freud put forth some theories as to why that might be true too, but we won't chase that rabbit just yet.

Clearly, almost from birth little girls are wired to approach life differently than do boys. And also clearly, young girls of our generation were taught by the adults in our lives to behave as "little ladies." Don't make waves, perfect those important social skills, always look attractive, be the flawless lady-in-waiting, ready to receive her Prince Charming as he rides up on his proverbial white horse to take care of us and live happily ever after in our two-story colonial house on Willow Lane.

Now can you picture the little turtle sprinting for the sea, and how desperate she must feel?

THE TORMENT OF ADOLESCENCE

"Biologically speaking, if something bites you, it is more likely to be female."
– Desmond Morris
(British zoologist, ethnologist and anthropologist)

Ah, adolescence. I suppose I can confess here that I always called these the "wonder years" when I was raising my children, as in "I wonder why I thought it was such a great idea to have children?" Of course, I don't mean that now, and I didn't mean it then. But I will say that those years, both in my memory of living through them myself and in trying to guide my children through them, were the most tumultuous, churning, anxiety-ridden, gut-wrenching times I can remember. Adolescence is the grinder through which we're all run to see what kind of person squeezes out on the other end, bloody and in a million pieces. Every phase of life is critical to a woman's development; this one, I believe, leaves the deepest scars, especially on girls.

Think about it. By the time a girl reaches adolescence, she's learned (for the most part) that she's not going to out-run or out-muscle most boys. In fact, and even scarier, she's learned that she really doesn't want to. During this stage of life, boys aren't so much the enemy any longer; in fact, they're sort of fascinating in a goofy, secret, intriguing way. It is, in fact, other girls who have become the adversaries, because other girls compete on a much more basic, ugly level than boys could ever hope to. For the most part, girls at this age are jockeying for social position, popularity, alliances, and of course, for boys. And if you've ever seen girls at this age interact for any length of time, you know exactly how cruel, how ruthless and vicious they can be. They can sometimes appear to be little sociopaths with budding breasts, garish beginner-applied makeup and hormones (always driving the roller-coaster, those hormones) that make them crazy on their best day. The icing on the adolescent cake is that this age brings on the start of menstrual cycles, a fact which either causes the sociopathy or exacerbates it, I haven't figured out which.

It will be years before adolescent girls understand just how upset God was with Eve when she committed her historic indiscretion with the fruit, but they will definitely learn that their menstrual cycles will come to rule their lives if they allow them to. Frankly, a woman's cycle will come to rule the lives of several key people in her life if she allows it, but that knowledge will come with the years, which are broken down into crampy, irritable, twelve-month increments. When the big event first hits, a girl becomes a woman (biologically), and life as she knows it will never be the same. She feels fear, excitement and wonder. She feels bloating and monumental inconvenience. She visits a new aisle at the supermarket once a month.

My mom, and countless others before her, referred to a menstrual cycle when speaking to her daughters in terms other than its scientific name – anything but that, please. My mother referred to it as "your time of the month." Other moms: "your delicate time." Delicate time? Of all the things I feel during this time each month, delicate is nowhere on the list. I feel irritable, swollen, weirdly resentful and generally awful during my "delicate time," but I do not feel at all delicate. One woman I interviewed actually had to endure her mother referring to her period as "Aunt Flo." Still others called it, more accurately, "the curse."

Young girls don't know what to do with any of the stirrings they feel during these early hormone-driven years. Some are thrilled to see their breasts start to emerge, and some are mortified. Overnight, blemishes set up camp on their previously clear faces. Everything's changing, inside and out. They're giddy one minute, morose and brooding the next.

Change is always a bit intimidating. Some girls begin very early on to feel the power of their sexuality, and still others never will. The changes in a girl's body at this age are vast, with lifelong effects. Every hormone-related metamorphosis leaves an indelible mark.

Incidentally, it's probably best that young girls have no idea how many opinions will be formed about them based simply on the eventual size of their breasts, those opinions usually formed by men but to their credit, not always. Large breasts get a man's attention, period. Large breasts are a good thing on Planet Man. Some say that the fascination traces all the way back to those early years of breastfeeding; others say that since men are visual creatures, large breasts are more visually stimulating than smaller ones. We could kick these theories around for hours but let's face it, the bottom line is that many a set of large breasts has opened many a door for many a woman (figuratively speaking, of course).

Conversely, they've probably closed a few doors, too. The flip side of this size-based theory is that large breasts can also lead both men and women to draw the foregone conclusion that a large-breasted woman possesses a less-than-impressive I.Q. Small breasts, on the other hand, have little to do with whether a woman is considered to be smart or ditzy. It makes no sense, but that's the reality, the large and small of it, so to speak.

This train of thought brings us to something else that's changed from the time our moms were young women to today, and that's our undergarments (our "unmentionables," as I've heard them called more than once on this journey). Back in the day when I was a little girl, secretly admiring my mother's beautiful and mysterious perfume bottles, there were a few times I'd get brave enough to open the drawer in her dresser that contained her unmentionables. Surprisingly, that drawer was not padlocked. As I believe I have already shared, my mother was well endowed, as were all of her German-descended sisters and most of her daughters, myself excluded.

I remember peeking into that secret drawer, handling and considering those white (always white, without exception) garments that had to have been designed during the Spanish Inquisition. Sturdy, reinforced and built to withstand industrial-grade pressure and force, my mother's bras were scary looking structures. There was no lace, there were no flowers, and there were no flirty, peek-a-boo keyholes. No hearts, no chains, no flirtatious writing. My mother's unmentionables were all business, built for all work and no play.

And let's not forget about the girdles. I got a glance at my mother, dressed only in her underthings, probably two or three times in my entire life, and then only by accident. I remember being in awe of the sheer power of what appeared at first glance to be just plain old fabric. Girdles, in my best guess, must have been constructed from some NASA-inspired amalgamation of steel, fiberglass and some token cotton. My mother was an attractive woman, but I do remember that, by the time she got fully dressed from her inner foundations to her final layer of business clothes, she looked like a well-dressed Italian sausage, with well-defined but smooth bumps and lines.

I never understood the thinking behind wearing a girdle. The law of physics dictates that one cannot, in fact, cram ten pounds of fat into a five-pound container without some of that fat sticking out somewhere else (and it's never in a flattering place, is it?). From what I remember seeing as a kid and in the years that followed, a girdle simply squeezed a woman like a wicked boa constrictor in some areas, just to spill the extra skin over unceremoniously into others. How uncomfortable my mother and millions of women like her must have been all day, every day, in their steel-reinforced white NASA casings.

Fast-forward to today, when women's lingerie is supremely feminine, absolutely fun and delightfully beautiful. I love pretty lingerie. I love the way it makes me feel, like wearing a very pretty, feminine secret. I like knowing that my husband, and no one else, knows I'm wearing it.

The thong (and I'm not talking about summer sandals), another tool of the Inquisition, is a squirmy exception to my love of all things feminine and unmentionable. I can't wear thongs. I don't understand how women do. The few times I've tried, I ended up spending half my day trying to dig the thin, stretchy floss out of secret places in my south forty - not a sexy, come-hither look if you ask me. Of course, my rear end probably isn't designed to wear a thong, but whose is? Barbie's, that's whose.

The other lacy, feminine underpinning I simply can't manage is one of those "wear it in a hundred different ways" bras. You know the kind; the bra is sold in one package, and the straps, fasteners, bungee cords, tie-downs and staples are packaged separately. I never could figure out the "hundred different ways," even though they look so easy and effortless in the catalogues. In fact, I never could figure out the one, normal way to wear it, as it never came pre-assembled. I couldn't figure out how to keep all the extra parts straight and stored with the correct bra, either. More often than not, our dogs used the stretchy treasures to play a very expensive version of tug-of-war.

More than once, I've gotten myself so hopelessly tangled up in one of those expensive harnesses that I had to call in reinforcements (usually my husband, but sometimes one of the girls) just to free myself. That's an embarrassing thing to admit, but it's true nonetheless. Who needs to wear a bra a hundred different ways, anyway? My wardrobe isn't that complicated. Nonetheless, I think the evolution of lingerie speaks volumes about the evolution of our attitudes about our bodies. A few short decades ago, the purpose of our underthings was to control, curb, hide and downplay our curves. Today, lingerie showcases what God (and sometimes talented surgeons) gave us. An entire industry has been built on this newfound pride in our physiques. All in all, I think the change is a healthy one.

This may sound strange, but I always encouraged our girls to wear pretty underthings. I wanted them to understand that their bodies were beautiful, made exactly as they were intended to be, and that wearing pretty, lacy things was something for them to enjoy. Pretty lingerie is not just packaging for a man to unwrap; wearing it can be a private expression of self-assurance and acceptance of our own bodies, something that's been in pitifully short supply down through the years.

I remember the first time I went bra shopping with my mother. I really didn't need a bra; she was just so accustomed to her other daughters being solidly in a "C" cup by the age of 12, she felt it was in my best interest to conform. Maybe she thought that saddling me up with a bra might stimulate some kind of glandular growth, I don't know, but when she decided it was time, it was time. There was no arguing the point. I was a late bloomer (in fact, I didn't fully bloom until I met a fabulous cosmetic surgeon when I was in my early forties), so I must have been, maybe, 12 or 13 years old at the time. Don't laugh. That's one of the many scars that only a mother – a Southern mother at that - can inflict with the deftness and dexterity of a skilled surgeon.

I come from a long line of German women who are built like curvaceous tanks. I don't know what happened to me. I got the "tank" gene, but the voluptuous curves ... well, suffice it to say that surgeons, not diamonds, can be a girl's best friends.

But back to bra shopping. My mother lectured me all the way from our house to Lenox Square in Buckhead (a tony section of Atlanta) about how proper young ladies wear, match and take care of their undergarments. "You can always tell a proper young woman by the way she keeps herself," she'd recite. I'd think to myself, "if the young lady is so proper, how would everyone know what her bra and underwear look like?" but with my mom, it was better to think those things than to actually say them out loud.

When we arrived at Lenox Square Mall, we headed directly to my mom's favorite department store, Rich's, a high-end Atlanta retailer that eventually morphed into Macy's. It was after all, her mother-ship; she had the credit card, a VIP parking spot and for all points and purposes, a personalized dressing room with monogrammed towels. My mom marched me right up to the clerk working the lingerie counter and exclaimed to her and everyone else in the entire mall that I FINALLY needed a brassiere.

Horrified, I froze as she solicited the opinions of other women who happened to be shopping in the same department. "What do you think? I think she needs to get into a bra now, don't you?" I could feel myself turning red all the way down to my toes, the heat of embarrassment rising against my painful modesty. The saleslady, this complete stranger, this woman on whom I had never laid my young eyes, peeked at me over her cat eye glasses, whipped out a tape measure and proceeded to wrap it around my chest. As my face burned scarlet red, I remember her snorting and snickering. Then Cat Eyes announced (again, to the entire third floor of the store) that we could probably wait on the bra but that if I wanted to "feel like a big girl," well then, over there was the AA training bra section (as she waved her well-manicured claw in the general area of training bras, like I was shopping for a bicycle instead of a brassiere).

The pristine, white, flat-cupped bras were no more than cotton circles held together with stretchy, adjustable straps. My mother picked up each and every one of them, held them up to my chest, and cocked one eyebrow, looking critically from my chest to my face and back again. I was sure she was wondering how on earth one of her girls could be so lacking in that particular area, but I fervently thanked God she never actually said it aloud in the store. After what seemed an eternity, my mother selected two AA-size bras, purchased them, and off we went. I was so relieved not to hear clapping from the audience in the lingerie section at Rich's, especially from Cat Eyes, the incorrigible tape-measuring Nazi. I believe that day was the first of many that had me wishing the floor at Rich's would open up and swallow me whole, AA training bra and all. Come to think of it, each and every time I wished that, I was shopping with my mother.

When all these physical and emotional changes begin to stir in a girl, when others begin to take notice of the physical changes in her, something significant happens. It did to me, and I think I can say with some accuracy it did to most of my friends. It has happened probably since the beginning of time. The changes begin to emerge, and girls begin to develop a dislike, dare I say even a hatred, of their own bodies. They become hyper-critical of the developments, and of how they are emerging. Too often, this loathing of our physical appearance continues well into adulthood. If we're tall, we wish we were shorter. If we're a D-cup, we wish for a B-cup; if we're a B-cup, we wish for a D. If our hips are broad or our legs too skinny, we long for the opposite. Very few women I've ever known are truly happy with their bodies. It takes a very long time to learn (if we ever do) that we can't fight our body types, but we can make sure that we keep them healthy with proper nutrition and exercise. Until we reach that line in life's sand, we strive to look exactly like those emaciated, gangly skeletons that grace the pages of fashion magazines for women of all ages. Heaven help us, Barbie has long been our pattern for what the perfect body looks like, and even she could be considered "fat" by today's models' standards.

Besides, if Barbie were a real woman, she would be so top-heavy she'd be confined to a wheelchair. And did it ever bother you - as it did me - that she didn't have any discernable means of earning money? She had condos and penthouses and sports cars, fabulous clothes and jewelry, but no job. Makes you wonder how she got all that stuff, doesn't it? Oh well; I'm sounding judgmental now. Let's get back to the female physique and the outlandish perceptions we have of it as women.

O.K. one more comment: It might have been nice if they had made "Muffin Top Barbie," or "Flat-chested Barbie." Who knows, maybe more young women would have developed acceptance of their bodies at an earlier age if those diverse, more realistic Barbies and others had existed.

I read an article a while back, one about a woman who loathed her own physique so much that, twenty years ago, she hired a photographer to take nude pictures of her in several tasteful positions, just so she could see what others were truly seeing when they looked at her. Her then boyfriend was very critical of her body, and like most women, she already had a terrible view of her own form. Surprisingly, she was both shocked and pleased when she received the photos – "I was beautiful," she remembered thinking, when she saw the graceful black and white photographs of her feminine curves and nearly flawless skin.

Twenty years later, when the same woman was well into her forties and had given birth to two daughters of her own, she was feeling very bad about her body once again. As a result, she had the same photos re-taken. Same positions. Nude. Black and white. She recalled again being shocked when she looked over the photos that reflected some very definite changes, but again she was pleasantly surprised when she saw those stark, honest pictures. What she saw were natural changes in the female body that come with age, of course. But she, and only she, could also see the wisdom, self-assuredness and contentment that were present in that second set of snapshots. Again, she saw beauty. It's amazing what we women conjure in our minds, distorted views of our own form and figure. Are they reflections of media and others' opinions, or do we conceive these negative images all on our own? I think maybe the answer is a combination of the two, and I know without a doubt the dislike first rears its ugly head during adolescence.

I've thought about this phenomenon an awful lot over the years, and I didn't realize until I was well into my forties my own personal struggle with this physical self-loathing with which I've wrestled most of my life. Why do we do it to ourselves? Maybe it is because so much emphasis is put on being perfectly pretty. Maybe it's because television and magazine ads make women look like perfect, airbrushed, starved goddesses. Maybe it's the fact that we internalize the cruel remarks made in the throes of our hateful, adolescent guttings. Whatever the reasons, we waste too much time being unhappy with our bodies, and it starts too early in life. Do boys, and later men, feel the same way about their bodies? I doubt it. I really do. They're coached to be strong, manly and assertive, but not pretty.

With our girls, my husband and I always told them they were pretty, yes, but we also high-fived academic achievement, athletic accomplishment, kindness, compassion and generosity. I'll admit, I've struggled to bite my tongue when I'd see them with their hair piled high atop their heads in a messy ponytail, no makeup on, and clothes looking like they were selected from a heap rather than from a closet. I haven't always succeeded in keeping my opinions to myself, but inwardly I was always very glad that they were confident enough and comfortable enough to be themselves rather than worry about who others expected them to be. I say I struggled with holding my tongue, because my knee-jerk reaction, well-rooted in my upbringing, was to critique and correct, even though I despised it when it was done to me. As I believe I have mentioned a hundred or so times, I was a chunky girl. I remember thinking to myself that I wished I had been born back in the days when beautiful women were depicted as plump, cherubic, curvy chicks, holding a harp in one hand and a turkey leg in the other. Even thirty-five or forty years ago, I was wishing I was someone else born in another time when in reality, I was simply ahead of my time.

How can I say that? Recently, I saw a short news story reporting to viewers that artists are now being hired to airbrush photos of models to make them look heavier. Again, there's that ever-changing mixed message that does nothing but confuse us, telling us what we are supposed to look like based on some imagined industry idea that changes from season to season, year to year, decade to decade and century to century.

I hope I've done a better job of encouraging self-confidence in our girls than my own mother did in me. In all honesty, our girls each struggled with body image to some degree, though I hope not to the extent that I and so many others have. But enough on that subject, until we get further down the road, anyway, and our bodies begin doing some pretty crazy things – yet again.

Some girls at this youthful stage of life are fascinated with a new-found hobby called "boys," and some are confused by it. Some girls just naturally know how to climb to the top of the social ladder (and that ladder is erected early in elementary school these days, not in middle or high school). Some girls just stand staring at the bottom rung, not knowing how — or maybe even why -- to take that first step. And swirling around and through this tornado of physical and emotional changes is some of the most cutting cruelty many will ever encounter. Why? Of course there are many theories surrounding why adolescent girls sprout claws and fangs and use them indiscriminately. I believe that, just as boys compete physically, girls compete emotionally, simple as that. The sad thing is that the wounds these young girls inflict never truly heal. Each one leaves a scar, large or small, deep or superficial, that takes one more nick out of the woman that girl will eventually become. Or maybe the scars add to the woman, who knows? Perhaps the outcome depends on the girl.

Consider this: Have you ever watched two boys get into a fight? It doesn't matter what the scuffle is about; it could be a game of basketball, who has to wash the dishes, who took the video game out of the box and didn't return it. It really doesn't matter. Later on in life, the fight could even be over a girl. The boys will fight like those wild animals you see on the National Geographic channel: punching, wrestling, swearing, kicking ... and when they're done, they're done. Just like that. Five minutes later, they're best friends again. That's always amazed me. I admire it. I don't understand it, but I do admire it.

A girl, on the other hand, will start a rumor if another girl has stoked her ire. Or she'll say something to publicly humiliate that girl. She'll exclude a girl from a group or an event, making sure that everyone knows the girl was excluded. Yes, some will get down and dirty and fight physically, but I think that's become a new low that happens more often today than used to be the case. We really didn't see girls physically fighting when I grew up, or at least I didn't. It simply wasn't done by young ladies.

This kind of behind-the-scenes girl-fighting, the emotional cut-throat kind, isn't over in a few minutes, either. Girls learn early on to hold grudges and never forget (remember the tapestry?). It's during this tumultuous stage of adolescence that girls learn to be as tough as nails, no matter how soft, unaffected or composed they may look on the outside. It's merely a matter of survival. Girls are much more effective bulliers than they're given credit for being. The emergence of social media has sped up the bullying while at the same time lending anonymity to the bully – a dangerous recipe. Several times a year, we see the tragic outcome on the evening news: a young person takes his or her own life as a result. Those are the worst-case results; millions more live and grow up wounded and scarred, alienated and miserable, because children at this age are so unrelentingly cruel and vicious. I firmly believe that girls are more adept at this type of bullying than boys can even imagine. It's a trait for which we're well known and of which I, for one, am not proud. It's a black eye on being what's otherwise a wonderful thing to be – a woman.

I'm reminded of another social experiment I learned about in high school, one in which a single young girl (let's call her Girl A) was purposefully, blatantly ostracized by a group of girls to the point of truly being terribly cruel. No one would befriend her; she had no one, not even one other girl friend, in whom to confide or with whom to cry. This treatment went on for weeks, and then a new element was introduced into the picture. Another girl (we'll call her Girl B), also ostracized, ridiculed and humiliated by the same group, only this time the group included Girl A in their circle, encouraging her to be cruel to Girl B. Our task in school was to write a paper predicting how Girl A would react. In my heart of hearts, I wanted to believe that Girl A would befriend Girl B. How do you think Girl A reacted?

I'll never forget my disappointment when our professor told us that Girl A jumped up on the bandwagon with the "mean girls" and treated Girl B just as cruelly as she herself had been treated. She was so thrilled that her mistreatment had stopped, so thrilled to be included in the group of mean girls, that she had no compunction about treating another girl the same way she had been treated. I was stunned, as I was sure she would have reacted differently, taken the second girl under her wing and befriended her, giving them both a friend and confidant. But it doesn't seem to work that way.

It's in our adolescent years that we learn to believe that "belonging" is more important than simply "being." Thankfully most of us outgrow that myth by the time we reach our twenties, but that's a long time to live your life and treat others according to that one flawed principle. It can be devastating, both to us and to others.

An adolescent girl's desire -- with rare exception her burning need – is to belong to a group, often at any cost. Up until this point in her life, that group has been her family. Now she sees other groups, membership in which can mean popularity with other girls, with boys, with teachers, with any group she wants. Sometimes, a girl is granted that membership; other times, she is not.

The tables have turned a bit in the years between when we were growing up (again, I'm talking about women in their forties and better). Boys, of course, were at the center of most of the silly things we did, but we were still encouraged to be "young ladies." In other words, promiscuity did not earn one popularity, at least not with other girls. Pretty much without fail, it didn't earn a girl brownie points with her parents, either. Even back then though, a promiscuous boy (yes, promiscuous) was a source of pride, at least for many dads. Today, so many parents look the other way because it's simply too difficult to discipline, too dangerous to risk actually angering one's child. It's my personal belief that today's parenting does not bode well for our country's tomorrow.

At any rate, then and now, being a loosely-moraled girl was a great plus for being popular with boys, but certainly not out in the open. When I was a young girl, promiscuous girls were very popular with boys on the sly, but boys rarely dated (or "took home to Mama") anyone but a "good girl." It's around this time in life – adolescence -- that girls begin to learn the hypocrisy of that conundrum.

Yes, a boy will tell a girl that sex is a very good thing – critical to his very existence at exactly the right moment – but if she gives in, just to hear later that he's told all his buddies about the experience (adding, no doubt, a few embellishments) and never calls or wants to see her again, she's learned a valuable lesson that too many girls learn way too early: Sex is a tool, and some boys are just skilled and deft salesmen. Of course eventually we learn another lesson, and that's that women initially have more emotionally invested in sex than men do (at least early on), but that's a lesson that's hard won, and it takes time to sink in.

No matter your generation, girls learn that sex is a very powerful utensil, wielded properly. I'm afraid that girls are learning it younger and younger and that's a shame, because not only is sex a tool, it's also a weapon in some very young hands.

In my generation (I'm in my glorious fifties), sex was basically a carrot, a prize to be dangled in order to achieve a goal. In my family, S-E-X was not discussed. "The talk" my mother had with my sister and me went pretty much like this: "Don't do it. You'll go blind, and people will talk." Then she handed us some medical brochures (with terrible illustrations, I might add) and went into the kitchen to cook dinner. My sister and I flipped through the brochures, then looked at each other as if to say, "If this is all there is to it, what's the big deal?" Suffice it to say that stick figures labeled "A" and "B" don't do the subject justice.

I never heard the word "pregnant" used in our home. A woman was "expecting," never "pregnant." As a young girl I used to wonder, "She's expecting? What? News? A prize? An important package?" I somehow knew better than to ask, but of course eventually I figured it out on my own.

In older generations, women in their sixties and up, sex was still a dangling carrot, but the horse was always walking true north, toward the altar, because that's where the carrot was headed. Period. That was the goal. If a girl slipped up and offered the carrot before reaching the altar and a baby ensued, everybody was still headed to the altar. That's just the way it was. For some women, the arrangement worked out and worked well. For too many others, a miserable marriage, bottomless resentment and unhappy children were the result, but divorce was still not an option.

And with sex at the center of everything and hormones zinging and bouncing off the walls, we enter the glorious teen years of female development.

THE TEEN YEARS - OR "MOM!"

"Next to the wound, what women make best
is the bandage."
– Jules Barbey d'Aurevilly
(French novelist and short story writer)

If I said often of my girls' adolescent years that they were the "wonder years," I said twice as many times, "Please God, give me strength" during their teen years. Teenage girls are a formidable cross between a rattlesnake, a flower, an angel and an angry badger. As a parent of one or more, you can only pray, hold on tight and love 'til it hurts, sometimes literally.

When I was a teen, I was more of a wallflower than anything else. I was a bookworm, a "late bloomer" as my mother reminded me (every chance she got, and as loudly as she could), and an introvert. I was too much of a book lover for my own good, and I was far too shy for my own good. I was torn between the advice I always heard –- to be sweet, to be attractive, to be gracious, not abrasive – and my innate desire to be taken seriously, to do something with my life that would leave its mark. In other words, I yearned to be me and not who everyone else insisted I be. Sounds very 1970s, I know, but it was indeed the 1970s.

To make things even worse, I can admit now that I remember always having a sense of inadequacy as a teenage girl. First, I was overweight (have I mentioned that?). In truth, I was not obese but slightly overweight, though the image in my head was grotesquely obese and then some. Overweight girls are treated by other teens (girls and boys alike) as lepers, as less-than-good-enough disposable creatures – walking targets for other kids and even well-meaning relatives.

Sounds harsh, maybe even a little dramatic, I'll admit. But if you struggled with being an overweight teenage girl, you also know it's pretty accurate. And while I was overweight and in retrospect, pretty in a young, clueless kind of way, my head painted a very different picture of my body. In my head, I was hideously fat, horrible to look at, and undeserving of just about anything.

Secondly, my mother died when I was seventeen years old, her last stop along the interminable journey through the hell known as leukemia. I understand that medical science has progressed by leaps and bounds in the more than thirty years since my mother died, but back then the cure seemed to be worse than the disease. She paid dearly for every day she lived past her diagnosis. Our home life was, to say the least, very different from my friends' lives. I never understood cliques, ostracizing, or what merited one's inclusion in a group.

I had other things to think about. Truthfully, I still don't understand cliques. For all practical purposes, I really didn't have a mom from about age 13 on. My mother was so sick, just getting through a day took all the presence of mind she possessed. To say that I felt different, odd and alone during those years would be pretty accurate, even while she was alive. I was wise beyond my years, and terribly naïve. When she died, my island got even smaller. Oh, the feelings that grieving requires us to slog through: anger, denial, sadness, and yes, even envy. I envied other girls who still had their moms; as I shared earlier, sometimes I still do.

I have three girls in my family, and of course all of them were teens at some point. Each one was different from the next, but they were all challenges. For years, I worried that I wouldn't know how to be a mom to a teenage girl (and let's face it, does anybody really know how?). Without a doubt, I made mistakes, but I hope that what the girls saw during that stage of life was that I loved them and wanted desperately to do all the right things, to teach them all they needed to know, and to protect them from the danger of poor choices and influences until they could see around those corners for themselves.

Not too long ago, my youngest daughter and I had a conversation about her not-too-distant teen years and the way she and I navigated them. Socially, we were about as opposite as two people could possibly be. She cheered football and basketball in high school. She dated cute, popular guys. During those years, I would watch her in fascinated amazement, loving her so much, yet feeling like I was hanging on for dear life – literally – trying to teach her life lessons without "ruining" her life in the process.

Isn't that what all teenage girls think their moms are put here on earth for, to ruin their lives? One of the sticking points between us was the fact that so many kids in her circle of friends (football players, cheerleaders, wrestlers) had parents who seemed to be afraid to actually parent their little darlings.

Drinking and drug use among this crowd was prevalent, and there were homes in which both were allowed for all of the high schoolers, a fact that still amazes me even as I write the words on this page. These were many of the popular kids, those whose opinions "mattered," those who rarely if ever heard the word "no" from mommy and daddy. All of her friends were allowed to drink, and when she was told that she was not allowed to go to the homes in which drinking was allowed, there was friction in our home and among her and her friends. She felt (and often was) ostracized.

Some of her girl "friends" turned on her like rabid dogs, and she learned some very tough lessons during those difficult years, the toughest of which was that friends, many times, were friends only when it was expedient. At the time, of course, she felt that my husband and I drew breath for the sole purpose of making her life difficult. She also learned that, during those confusing, viciously cruel girl-eat-girl years, friends came and went with the wind.

Anyway, when she and I had a long conversation about the difficult situation years after this all happened, she said she understands now that we were just trying to protect her, to teach her that right is right, no matter

who's in the room. She learned that standing for something can be a very lonely undertaking.

I learned something too, and that's that not parenting a child is oh-so-much easier than parenting a child, and today that's the path that too many parents take. An alarming number of parents allow their children to make the wrong choices because they want to be their child's best friend, not their parent. That makes it hard for the rest of us to teach our children values and life lessons about choices, consequences and responsibility. My insistence on respecting and teaching laws and common sense ended up alienating my youngest daughter in high school. The peer pressure to conform was suffocating. I didn't fully understand what she went through until we had this recent talk. I sound like I'm preaching, I know, but I'm just remembering how hard those years were for us and for her. They didn't have to be.

I believe teenage girls are so difficult, especially with their moms (and of course stepmoms), because they are becoming young women themselves and as we all know, two women cannot live under the same roof for long. Teen girls cut their teeth on their mothers, but if we just hang in there long enough, we become friends with our daughters again. My girls are fun to be around these days, because they've grown up and I've mellowed. It's a hard-earned friendship, but one to be treasured for a lifetime.

Women are strong-willed. We first realize this when we are teenagers, in my opinion. Gone is the adolescent child who patterned her every move after someone she wanted desperately to emulate (usually some awful kid at school because she knew her mom would hate that). Replacing her is this being, this woman-child who fluctuates between the desire to remain a carefree child and running the inevitable race toward adulthood.

Our mom's advice and admonishments, once the center of our universe, begin sounding intrusive and overbearing. The more Mom tries to teach, the harder a teenage girl digs in her heels and resists. It's just the way of the world, God's manner of preparing a young woman to go out and make her own home, make her own way, and take no prisoners. Personally, I also believe it's His way of helping Mom let go when it's time to let go.

During this hormonal, jerky, roller-coaster jaunt we call the teen years, self-expression is paramount, although a teen's self-expression is often an expressed yearning to just belong to a group. Sometimes, any group will do.

It's no secret that one of the ways a teen girl expresses herself is by the way she dresses. Her clothes say an awful lot about her before she ever opens her mouth to tell you that you're wrong. A girl may be preppy; she may be gothic (you know, the black hair, black clothes, black fingernails, everything); she may be a throwback to the 60s; she may be artsy; she may be sharply academic. She may be funny and outgoing, shy and reserved, or a raving witch. At this age, a young woman's self-expression buds and blooms. She and others get their first real, true glimpse of what matters to them, and they find a way to express it.

The teen years are also the time when many young women come to a fork in the road, or one of their first, anyway. During this time, the fascination we had with boys in adolescence has evolved into -- for some -- a need to constantly be attached to one. Some girls see being half of a couple as crucial to what defines them. I knew (still do), and I'm sure you did too, girls who could not function, who did not feel whole without being somebody's girlfriend. I knew girls like that, and my girls have known girls like that. In fact, I know grown women who are still like that.

There are theories that claim that this phenomenon results from a poor father/daughter relationship, and that may be true. More fundamentally, I think the need to be attached to a man is rooted in poor self-worth. What matters most, though, is not why some girls feel pressured to be attached to a guy; it's what these girls are willing to trade for that yearning to belong, and this time to a boy or a man. Teen pregnancy rates and STDs speak to this very question. In the heat of passion, a girl's life can turn on a dime, can be forever altered by the coming of a child. Yes, I know that there are boys who promise to – and do – "man up," so to speak and take on the responsibilities of fatherhood while still children themselves. But a boy's life never changes as drastically as the girl's in this situation. And that's just the simple truth, no matter how you slice it.

A girl trades something else, too, for the privilege of being called someone's girlfriend. Even if she chooses to become sexually active but never gets pregnant, the girl has made a trade, because sex (especially the first time) is a colossal event to her, even if she tries to appear nonchalant about it. In our society today, in which sex is treated so casually, it still matters to a young woman, deep down inside where she is timidly still learning about womanhood, the first time she gives herself away.

I saw a fascinating documentary a few years ago, and the subject of and conclusions made in this film have never left me. The filmmaker was following the course of this country's attitude toward sex from the early 1900s through today. The portion of the film that really made an impression on me was the one that dealt with the 1920s, the "Roaring Twenties," as many historians refer to that period. Many young people who lived during that time were stepping out, getting turned on to jazz music, that free, sexy rambling of riffs and runs and wildly sexy musicians that became so popular among young people that the term "jazz craze" became more than just a musical reference.

When young people (particularly women) behaved "loosely" or "scandalously," following these musicians around and letting their hair down in bedrooms all over the country, being "jazz crazed" actually became a psychological and legal defense of these same young women when they got into trouble.

Also, during that period of time, when a young woman (or even an unmarried adult woman) engaged in premarital sex, she not only brought shame on herself, she brought it on her family. Having raised my children in the permissive climate in which we now live, in a world of so many young people who view sex in much the same way as my Jurassic generation viewed hand-holding or kissing, the changes are astounding.

The contradictions are still there (a girl who's known to "do it" is still considered a "slut" by her peers, make no mistake), but a whole lot more of them are "doing it" anyway. Being a slut, as it turns out, isn't that bad if you ask some girls today. It's no big deal. No wonder we grow up confused by our maturation, hating our bodies and utterly confused by sex, often engaging in it long before we are emotionally ready to do so.

When a young girl feels she must belong to a boy at all costs, she trades herself. She loses herself to someone else, because belonging to another person at any cost is the ultimate trade: her "self" for his. Her interests for his. Her dreams and goals for his. Her identity for his.

Anyway, back to sex and the mixed messages we're fed our entire lives. Remember this one?

"Why buy the cow if you can get the milk for free?"

Unfortunately, that was one of my mother's favorites. I always found this one to be rather offensive. Cow? Really? But the thinking behind this adage is that sex (again, a tool) should be withheld until the boy/man closes the deal and marries the girl/woman first. Sex is "the milk," and marriage is the act of "buying the cow." No wonder we have skewed views about the whole thing. I can't even look at a gallon of milk to this day without feeling both confused and offended, and maybe even a little turned on.

I hope I have done a better job with my girls in teaching them about sex, marriage, commitment and self-worth. I always tried to approach the delicate subject of sex and whether and when to do it from the angle of self-respect and self–esteem. Having raised my children in a very hands-on manner, I knew better than to bury my head in the sand and pretend that they would not be presented with this puzzle early on in life. And yes, I had a similar talk about choices and responsibility with my son. I tried to be as honest as I could without being the cause of added years of therapy down the road, but it's a tricky topic laced with opportunities for damaging your kid forever. On this subject, words must be chosen wisely. It's a mine field.

I tried the open, honest, brutally frank approach to the subject with my youngest daughter. She's the one, I used to jokingly say, for whom the oldest three were preparing me. Sharp, inquisitive and never resting until she was satisfied that she got the truth and nothing but, she would not allow me to sugar-coat the topic of sex. Or Santa. Or half-price sales. Or divorce. Or life and death. She never allowed me to skirt heavy topics or even to use euphemisms. I believe she was in the sixth or seventh grade when we acknowledged and addressed the scantily-clad elephant in the room, commonly known as S-E-X.

I made the mistake of telling my daughter that God would not have made sex such a beautiful, enjoyable expression of love without protecting it — and us — by putting parameters around it. He created sex to be beautiful, even enjoyable, I told her in my best "let's-talk-frankly, just-us-girls" voice, for a man and a woman to share under the right circumstances. I cringe even now recalling the conversation and the (in hindsight) woefully inadequate words I offered up.

I knew it would never fly for me to tell her what my mom told me, that sex is awful and will make you go blind. She'd never buy it. "You will only have one first time," I added, foolishly thinking that logic and common sense might somehow play a role in this conversation.

As I should have predicted, my words backfired. What she heard and what I thought I said were two totally different conversations. She was nauseated by my careful choice of words, traumatized, horrified that I would allude to the fact that I could possibly have ever enjoyed sex, with anyone, especially my husband, ever, under any circumstances. But I could see that she was digesting the information and the monumental nature of the matter amid all the protests, jokes (I told you before, she's a lot like me) and claims of stomach-churning nausea.

For the record, I did not once, ever, ask her why one would buy the cow if one could get the milk for free, so at least give me that.

Girls today are faced, I believe, with an even tougher landscape than our generation was. When we were teens, at least in theory, girls who "did it" were not good girls, and there was an air of taboo around sex and girls who partook before marriage. It was a hypocritical line in the sand, but it was at least a line.

Today, the general attitude among many young people with regard to sex is that it's no big deal, more of a pastime than anything else. There is no line. I think there's harm in that attitude, because it *is* a big deal. It's a huge deal. It's a staggering, life-changing deal, especially for young girls. "Free milk" is never really free.

But let's assume that a young woman navigates those teen waters successfully and avoids a too-soon pregnancy or other life-changing consequence. Something that is more true for girls today than ever before is the fact that they actually have choices with respect to career or vocation, and serious preparation begins in their teen years. Secondary schools now expect teen girls to prepare for life after high school. They encourage and guide young girls toward that goal.

When I was in high school, girls were offered Typing and Home Economics in addition to the general academic courses. Of course, we could take the higher maths, and I did, but frankly I never correlated those courses with future and career. Math really wasn't my thing. It still isn't. Ask my husband.

I was terrible at typing. I never did get the hang of it. I still type with just two fingers. I was terrible at Home Economics, or at least with the sewing part of it. It took me three months to make an apron, and I had to secure the hem with masking tape and glue in order to finish the project on time and earn a GPA-tanking "D" for my effort. So I guess it's safe to say that "Home Ec" wasn't my thing, either.

My lack of prowess in these areas worried me a bit, because my mother had always admonished her daughters to learn typing and shorthand so that we could support ourselves until we married someday. "Pay attention in Home Ec, because a good woman knows how to make a good home," piggy-backed that advice. Based on my high school performance in those areas, I had a dim vision of myself living on the streets, never able to get a job that required typing, wearing clothes with no hems, and starving to boot.

As it turned out, when I went on my very first job interview after graduating college with honors and diving head-first into graduate school courses, the first question the interviewer (a man) asked me was, "How fast do you type?" My heart sank.

Fortunately, young women today have the same educational and professional expectations and opportunities as do young men. All of my girls knew that college, if they chose to take their education further, was in their future. It was never "if." It was always "when." As it turned out, the oldest daughter chose to go, the middle daughter chose not to go, and my youngest girl is still going. Each of them made their decisions on their own terms and for their own reasons.

Linda, 58 years old and one of my interview subjects and beachcombing buddies I met while writing this book, was one of eight children. "We always knew that if Mom and Dad could afford school for any of us, my brothers would be the ones to go," she said. "That was just understood, because they would be the ones responsible for taking care of their families someday."

I'll note here that Linda, like so many other women I interviewed, was thrown in to the situation of losing her husband to cardiac arrest at a tragically young age. In other words, she did end up taking financial care of her family by herself for several years until the last child was grown. At that point, of course, she was responsible for supporting herself financially. The more women I spoke with, the more I came to understand that there must be very few of us who navigate life and end up financially secure because a man made us that way, at least without having to die to do it.

In summation then, if you are a teen, hold off on sex (there's no rush, believe me, it's not going out of style, and you and your true love did not invent it), listen to who your heart tells you you are, and feel free to express it while respecting yourself above all else. Make choices because you want to make them, not because others tell you to make them in order to fit in. Work as hard as you can in school so that you have many paths from which to pick and choose, as education translates into choices.

And as an added bonus to any teens who might by chance be reading this, tattoos are rarely a good idea in the long run (think sag, arm flab and droop in thirty or forty years), and be more selective about the music to which you listen. Any "artist" who refers to women as "bitches" and "hoes" can't be improving your quality of life that much, now can he?

BEING TWENTY, AND LEAVING THE NEST

*"I've yet to be on a campus where most women
aren't worrying about some aspect of combining
marriage, children and a career. I've yet to find one
where many men were worrying about the
same thing."
- Gloria Steinem
(American feminist, author and activist)*

By the time a young woman leaves her home,
the "nest" as we love to call it, she's likely ready. I
know my girls were. They talked and dreamed about
their own homes for years before they actually made
them. I think it's just natural – again, it's the way we're
wired. She may be leaving for college. She may be
leaving to marry. She may be leaving to travel or to live

with a man or with friends, or she may be leaving just because it's time. With her, she takes the life experience she's gained thus far, Mom's advice, Dad's love (and in the best case scenario, his advice too), hopefully a healthy dose of self-esteem, and a strong work ethic.

Women in their twenties can have the world at their feet today if they desire, at least as far as their options and choices are concerned. That's not always been the case. Just a few short decades ago, a woman's choices were sadly limited: marriage or spinsterhood.

Even in the early 1980s, I know I didn't feel ready or equipped for much of anything. I felt unsure, afraid of the prospect of being alone, and more anxious than excited about my future. Clueless, basically. My own worst enemy. Part of that anxiety can be chalked up to the fact that I was only 19 when I graduated college, part was just my nature, and part of it was because I wasn't following the confusing map my mother had laid out in the few short years she lived while I was a teenager.

I couldn't type. I didn't heed my family's advice to teach or go into law or accounting ("Because you'll never make a living writing books"), and I didn't particularly want to marry. However, as my beautiful young friend Alison reminded me not too long ago, some of us heard from our mothers and grandmothers:

"Never let anyone sweep beneath your feet, or you'll become an old maid."

This tidbit of wisdom, of course, leaves the taste in one's mouth that being an old maid might be a bad thing. Today, we call old maids well-adjusted, successfully single women; it's just a matter of perspective.

So I did marry, of course, at the ripe old age of 20, and the union ended disastrously a couple of years later. I'm embarrassed to say that in my mind, marriage was the next logical step in my life. I had graduated college, and marriage was next on my checklist. I married the man I happened to be dating at the time, which I suppose made the process all the more convenient for me. None of that pesky "finding the right guy for me" business to worry about. We were too young; our marrying was akin to putting two toddlers in the same playroom and expecting them to share and get along -- for three years. Up until I married my current husband, I had always made terrible choices where men were concerned. Oh my first two husbands weren't bad people (O.K. well maybe one was); we just weren't right for each other. We were too immature and selfish to understand concepts like "compromise" and "selflessness."

In my case the third time, as they say, was the charm. I'm not proud of that fact. I made the right choice with my current husband because I finally knew me, and I knew what I wanted. It took me nearly 40 years to figure those two ingredients out. In my opinion, marriage should not be an option for people under the age of 30 but as I said, I made very poor choices for almost four decades.

As a young woman in my twenties, I just didn't feel equipped for anything, didn't feel that I fit into any of the molds that had been forged for me. And I was seeing over and over again that my mother's advice, scant but well-intentioned, didn't really apply to my life with respect to career and marriage. I suppose I felt adrift; yes, that's a good word for it. And by the time I was 18, she wasn't around to answer any questions I might have had. I was ad-libbing and in hindsight, I was doing a pretty poor job of it.

I've always wondered whether I was alone in those feelings, whether other women my age had the same insecurities. Of course, the answers are, "No, you weren't" and "Yes, they did." In gleaning the material for the backbone of this book, I spoke with approximately forty women, all of them ranging in age from about thirty-five to eighty-eight. About a third of them had graduated college. Almost half of them went to college, but some never finished their post-secondary educations, primarily because they got married and supported their husband through his. Even thirty years ago, when a college couple married, it was often the woman who went to work full-time to help her husband complete his education. Fair? No, but that was just the way it was.

Of those women I interviewed who had dropped out of college early on, all but one had gone back to school later in life to complete her college education. Some did it while their children were young, and some waited until a bit later in life, but they did it because it mattered to them. For a couple of these women, it was simply a matter of principle. Not surprisingly, the number one career for which these women were preparing themselves was teaching, one of the few careers that's truly family-friendly. Incidentally, I'd like to point out here that some of the women were good typists, but most were hunt-and-peck, like me. Just throwing that out there.

I asked these women if they could recall their feelings, not their actual choices, but their *feelings* about dating, marriage and career during their twenties. Without exception, all of them said that dating, if they weren't already married, was a priority. After all, said Mom,

"You have to kiss a lot of frogs before you find your prince,"

and how could any of us ever forget these words of wisdom:

"You can fall in love with a rich man just as easily as you can a poor one."

The point here is that both men and women are in prime dating territory while they're in their twenties.

Dating is just what twenty-somethings do. The timing is right. It's fun. You have the time, the drive and the inclination to date at this stage of life.

Interestingly enough, as women (those who've come and gone, myself, and women for generations to come) progressed through their twenties, and whether they were married or not, another very important urge reared its head – a feeling, even an urgency, to bear children. The biological clock is a very real timepiece, as big and insistent as the one the crazy rabbit carried in *Alice in Wonderland*. It ticks loudly and unrelentingly from, say, our mid-20s up to age 40, maybe even a few years longer if we haven't already had children. If we have, that belligerent clock has likely been silenced by the noise our kids are making anyway.

The biological clock cannot be relegated just to older generations. It is timeless, so to speak. As for myself, I began to look at any man I dated as a potential father when I was in my twenties, certainly during the last year or two of college. It's not that I wanted to get married right then, but you have to start shopping for an important dress well before you make the actual purchase, right? Just reading that statement makes me cringe, but I vowed to be honest here even if it hurts. My mind just automatically went there when I was that age – to "would he make a good husband" territory - and believe me, I know how that sounds. Desperate. Remember, my marriage to my first husband ended when I was 23 or 24 years old. When I began dating again, the clock was ticking, clanging actually, banging me on the head, and it was very hard for me to ignore. Everything back then seemed so urgent, didn't it? Oh, if we had only known.

The point is that the vast majority of women have that clock. Of course, I've heard some women say that they do not and never did, and I have no doubt that that's true. But most of us do, and we have to plan our lives accordingly. I waited until I was 28 years old to have my first child, and I had my second at age 31. Those are prime career years and prime biological clock years. However, if you start having children in your early twenties, your career is also impacted and may sputter and falter before getting off the ground (if in fact it ever does). Some women wait until their mid-thirties or even early forties to have their babies, when their careers are steadily gaining traction or pretty well established. In this case, a woman conceives a child always with the knowledge that waiting that long increases exponentially the possibility of birth defects, problem pregnancies and other very serious considerations.

Do men think about any of this? I'm guessing not. All they have to do in a pinch is marry a younger woman, if they even give it that much thought. They can father children for, I don't know, a 70-plus-year timespan. Not much pressure there. Again, I am not man-bashing; these are just the realities circling this issue. Women have to think about children and career, agonizing over the questions of timing and the ability to make it all work. Truthfully, I can't say I can remember, nor have I heard from any of the women who have shared with me for this book, any memorable sayings or words of advice from Mom on this subject. There has to be a reason for that. Either our moms didn't have to balance career and children, or (as I suspect) there are no pat words to assist us in making these decisions, and no matter a woman's vocation, she has to make them.

I recall quite vividly one day a few years back, when I was driving to some appointment or another early one morning. I forget where I was going at the time; it really doesn't matter. I saw what I like to refer to as a live portrait, a snapshot that told a thousand stories. Have you ever done that, caught a glimpse of someone doing something that makes you wonder what led up to that exact action and point in time? I do, and often.

The image I spotted that day has never left me. I was sitting at a red light and happened to glance over to my left, where I saw a woman standing in the rain at the corner bus stop, waiting with her two young boys for the school bus. The three were all huddled under an umbrella. She was wearing a waitress uniform and glancing nervously (but not too obviously) at her watch every few seconds. I mentally filled in the blanks. This mom, who obviously works a very tough job and is worried about being late to it, was taking the time to wait with her boys and get them safely on the bus. She was stressed, but she was still there. She was juggling and balancing, worrying and caring, anxious and comforting – all of those skills that we women learn strictly out of necessity. That one scene, in my mind, sums up most succinctly a woman's choices and priorities, and the never-ending anxiety and responsibility that come with them. We are constantly pulled and torn.

Another first that most of us get to experience in our twenties is actually making our own home. Whether it's a college residence or first apartment or marriage nest, this is an exciting time for us. Finally, we get to put our own touch on our environment, and here's another area in which Mom can either come in handy or drive us crazy. My mother didn't live long enough to see this with her younger two daughters, but so many women have shared their experiences with me on this subject that I feel as though I lived it myself.

I opined earlier that two women can't, simply can't, co-exist under the same roof for very long. We mark our territory by decorating, arranging, painting and fluffing. I had a good laugh on this very topic with a charming woman, a retired school teacher named Stella, not too long ago. I met her on the beach when I was writing this book. She and three lifelong friends were spending a week together *sans* spouses, and they invited me to join them and spontaneously interview each of them. Of course, rather than conducting a formal group interview, we just sat in the sand, drank some very good wine, talked and laughed. Stella recounted her experience with her mother when she first moved in to her own apartment. "I was so proud of the place. It was probably a grand total of 400 square feet, but it was all mine," she remembered. "It was awful. I decorated with milk cartons and boxes and slipcovers and cheap paintings, but I loved it. I paid the rent, and I loved it." She then went on to tell me how, every time her mom came to visit, they had a ritual: "She'd call first, to give me time to 'pick up,' as she called it. Then, as soon as she walked in the door, she'd start moving things around, usually using just her index finger and thumb, as if everything she touched was crawling with bacteria. Then, she'd start cleaning. I'd move my things back where they were, never saying a word to her about it. We waged that silent battle for years and even today, she does that when she visits us in our home and stays in the guest room. She only rearranges the guest room, no other area. I think it's her way of giving in but still making a statement," she laughed. And Stella was probably right. We women rarely completely give in without making a clear statement, do we?

With all these things to consider and solve and decorate, then, we have one more really big crossroad that often materializes in our twenties, and that's choosing a husband. Not hunting, not trapping (as older generations often viewed the process), but choosing a husband. On this subject, my mother would tell us girls,

"Never date a man you wouldn't marry."

I used to think that was an odd thing to say, but I get it now. Unfortunately, what I think I understood her to say back then was, "Never date a man and not marry him." Three husbands later, I finally figured out what she meant. Better late than never, right?

What she intended to communicate to us was that a woman should set the bar as high as she chooses and never lower it, or date under it, so to speak. Expect to be treated well, to be respected, to spend time with a man who has both his and your interests at heart. Expect to marry a man whom you can love completely, raise children with, make a home with. In order to do this, however, a woman must know and understand herself first. Oh and all that glitters, is most definitely not gold.

When I was in college, there was a guy whom every girl I knew wanted to date. He was handsome, magnetic and Lord help us, he was pre-Law. In other words, he was the total catch. Imagine my surprise and excitement, then, when he caught up with me after class one afternoon and asked me out on a date that following weekend, to a Billy Joel concert, no less. I was absolutely giddy and more than a little proud of the fact that, of all my girlfriends and sorority sisters and all the other thousands of possibilities on campus, he had asked me out. As the date approached, my roommate and I planned and re-planned everything – my clothes, my hair, even right down to what we'd talk about (or how I'd answer when he talked about certain things).

When the big night arrived, I was nervous but felt prepared for anything. We went to the concert, then out to a very nice dinner, and before he took me back to the dorm, we took a stroll around the Bell Tower on campus. Legend was, if your date took you there for a stroll, well, he really liked you; you were destined to become a couple. I was beaming inside.

We took our stroll around the legendary campus quad, then he paused at a picnic table, climbed up and invited me to sit next to him. "Oh my gosh," I thought. "He's going to kiss me." If I had had my trusty notepad handy, I would have already been doodling my first name and his last, with one of those sickening curly-que hearts encircling the whole mess.

What he did, however, I still remember like it was yesterday. He leaned in, opened his mouth slightly, then laid his head on my chest and whispered, "You have no idea what a sense of security this gives a guy." My mind scrambled to translate that into, "I really like you. Would you like to kiss me?" It wasn't translating. My decoder wasn't working. Houston, we have a problem.

We sat there like that for what seemed like hours (though in hindsight it could have only been a few minutes) with me looking around in a panic to see if anyone I knew was also taking the legendary stroll. What was this guy doing? Going to sleep? Missing his mommy? I didn't know what to say or do, so I just sat there and waited for him to say something, to do something. Finally, he lifted his head, climbed off the picnic table, helped me down, and we walked back to my dorm. He looked positively satisfied, and I'm sure I looked positively puzzled. The moral of the story: Just because it walks like a pre-Law catch and talks like a pre-Law catch, doesn't necessarily mean it's either.

We went out a few times after that (me strictly out of curiosity, to tell you the truth), and as I suspected, this guy was a Mama's Boy extraordinaire. When he told me she ironed his underwear and shipped it to him weekly, that was the last straw, believe you me.

I have related that same advice about not dating a man you'd never marry to my girls because, quite simply, I do want them to set the bar high — very high. And as I learned first-hand from Mr. Pre-Law himself, not everyone is who they may seem to be at first. In other words, and this is a piece of advice I heard many women recite from their mamas:

"It is the woman who chooses the man who will choose her."

Being Twenty and Leaving the Nest

Or as some of our moms put it:

"Let a man chase you until you catch him."

The first version sounds so much better, don't you think?

And with all these things to juggle and balance and carry – striking out on our own, dating and marrying, listening to and eventually heeding the biological clock, we feel our way through our twenties.

BEING THIRTY AND FABULOUS...AND EXHAUSTED

"If a woman is sufficiently ambitious, determined and gifted, there is practically nothing she can't do."
- Helen Lawrenson
(American writer)

Crossing the threshold from age twenty-nine into age thirty is a milestone, and many women I know had a hard time with it. Thirty. It sounds so serious, so established. So no-nonsense. And by this age, a lot of women do indeed have their feet set on the path they intend to follow throughout life. Note that I said "intend" to follow. As we are already learning by this age, the best way to invite upheaval is to make definite plans.

Nevertheless, by this stage of the game we have chosen to be at-home moms, moms with careers, or career women with no children. We've chosen to be married or single. Suffice it to say that with all the birth control options out there for women, hopefully the choices with respect to reproduction have been conscious ones.

When I was younger than thirty, I remember thinking that that age sounded so old, so ancient. Practically dead. I think back now, twenty-plus years the other side of thirty, and chuckle at that idea. Women are just hitting their strides in their thirties, no matter which path they've chosen. We develop and fine-tune our multi-tasking skills. We work (and again, no matter whether you're an executive, a full-time mommy or a coffee shop waitress, women share so many common struggles). We parent and nurture, we strive to succeed professionally, we likely take care of the house or manage the arrangements to do so, and we also nurture (and yes, sometimes parent) our husbands. As our children reach school age, we PTA, we carpool, we serve as team mom and/or coach. We go to parent/teacher meetings. We help with homework. We listen and advise with respect to squabbles with friends, bullying, and not making the team. Sure, some dads do pitch in and lend a hand, but the buck ultimately stops with Mom. It did in the home I grew up in, anyway.

All of these responsibilities fall to us, unless we happen to be married to a man who is progressive-minded enough to believe he shares duties outside his workplace. Those men are out there; I know, because I married one. I also know they're rare. But if you do happen to have a husband who rolls up his sleeves and participates in getting things done at home, this is where we, women, need to give them a break and more than a little leeway.

It took me a long time to learn that everything pertaining to our children didn't have to be done exactly the way I'd do it myself. My (current) husband was terrific when it came to pitching in and doing the girls' hair, helping get all of the kids ready for school, or packing up snacks for the soccer team at halftime. I had to learn that, if he was taking care of a particular responsibility, I had to let him, and let him do it his way. If the girls left the house with zip-ties holding their ponytails, I learned to bite my tongue and thank him for his help. If the halftime snack cooler was packed with chocolate doughnuts and ZIP! Cola, I learned to thank him for taking care of that task and freeing up some of my time. If he took the initiative to handle dinner on nights when he got home from work before I did, I had to learn that frozen pizza or cinnamon rolls with sausage weren't going to kill anybody (served in moderation, of course). And if bath time at night left the bathroom looking like an automatic car wash, well, so be it. I and many other moms I talked to had to learn to loosen the reins and let Dad do the things he did the way he chose to do them. Yes, I even learned to be truly grateful for his contribution, not critical of it.

It was when I was in my thirties that the career/children conundrum was most difficult. My children were very young, and even before their father and I divorced I was, for all practical purposes, a single parent. If one of my children got sick at school and I was at work, it was my responsibility to make arrangements to leave work and care for him. Looking back, it seems that those years were filled with either looks of disapproval from my boss or the guilt of not being everything at all times to my children. The stress, it seemed, was always palpable.

For a time, my children were in daycare. It was my responsibility to drop them off and pick them up every day. For anyone out there who has had the same duty, I don't have to tell you about the agony of having a daycare worker peel a screaming child off of you while you promise that "mommy will be back soon." There were many days when I drove into Atlanta, battling bumper-to-bumper traffic, crying my eyes out and feeling like the worst mom in the world. We moms rarely cut ourselves a break.

Susan, a dear friend who so kindly shared her experiences with me, recounted a story that I found both familiar and hilarious, and so very true. We were talking about the difficulty of keeping all the balls in the air with respect to work and family and household during this phase of our lives, and she reminded me of one more responsibility we have as wives, moms, employees, drivers, coaches, counselors, nurses, et al.

"I can remember so many days, practically pulling my hair out from stress, rushing home to put dinner on the table (that's Southern for "prepare the evening meal"), get the house somewhat straightened up, help the kids with their homework, then nag all of them into bathing and going to bed. Just when I'd get the chance to sit down and put my feet up, here would come (my husband), kissing on my neck, wanting to hug and play and 'go upstairs.' Sex was the last thing on my mind!" Incidentally, "go upstairs" was this couple's double-secret code phrase for "have sex." Most parents coin such a phrase out of necessity. I'm sure you've heard a few creative ones over the years. One couple actually used the term, "do laundry." As if laundry isn't chore enough all on its own; simply calling sex "doing laundry" would have been a huge turn-off for me. Might as well call it root canal or gutter cleaning.

It's really true, though. Women are expected to wear dozens of hats during the day, a push-up negligee and fishnets in the evening, and have the boundless energy and burning desire for all of it, all of the time. So many women with whom I talked (especially us baby boomers) said that, not long after children came along, lovemaking became just one more thing to check off the to-do list. And that brings us to another nugget of wisdom shared from one generation of women to the next:

"Never tell your husband no."

Many of the women with whom I spoke, especially women age sixty and up, had heard this one, if not from their mothers then from aunts, grandmothers and family friends. When compiling all the conversations I had chronicled and collected for this book, I was struck by both the contrasts and the surprising similarities among all age groups of women with regard to attitudes about sex from then to now. Let me explain by sharing another anecdote with you.

Rosemary, a delightful woman who is now well into her eighties, was kind enough to share with me many of her personal accounts and hand-me-down advice. She and her husband were married for more than thirty years and had six children together; she lost him to cancer many years ago and never remarried. She told me something though, a story that I had a hard time understanding until she explained it fully. Her husband travelled quite a lot in the '50s and '60s, when their children were young.

"Oh, he had other women; I always knew that," she confided. "We just never talked about it, and he always came home. It was just his way. "

I had a hard time with that one. I wanted to ask her how she could have tolerated such treatment and have a shred of self-respect left, when she answered the question for me before I could even open my mouth: "I had six children and didn't have a paying job. What could I have done? And I would certainly never take his children and leave him alone." Besides, as she added, divorce was a big deal back then, not nearly as prevalent as it is today. Divorced women were treated, at least by other women, as though they were diseased and contagious. Husbands were not allowed to be alone with divorced women, because of course everybody knew they were constantly on the prowl for another life mate. Couples simply did not divorce unless under the most extreme circumstances. Infidelity, apparently, did not fall under the category of "extreme."

I understood Rosemary's predicament, but the idea of knowing what she knew — what so many other women must have known about their marriages, I'm sure — and looking the other way just didn't sit right with me. I was indignantly furious for her. Her matter-of-factness about his philandering floored me; it flustered me for a bit. It made me angry with her and for her.

Of course, many women today find themselves in the same boat; when we make the choice to work at home rather than outside the home (and we all know that "staying home," raising children and managing a home are never-ending work), we are also making the choice to be financially dependent on our husbands. There's an element of vulnerability there, and as Rosemary so eloquently illustrated for me, a terrible trade of sorts. In a perfect world, that wouldn't be true. But our world is not perfect, is it, and this terrible trade is but one of many a woman makes in her lifetime.

It's also in our thirties that yet another stark contrast between men and women begins to take shape, to manifest itself. This difference helped me understand another often-shared piece of advice passed from one generation to the next. I've always liked it and have shared it with my girls, as it explains so much about the struggles married couples encounter:

"A man marries a woman thinking she'll never change, and a woman marries a man thinking, 'Oh I can change him.' They both end up disappointed."

I have no idea who originally uttered that one, but isn't it the truth? I happened to have heard it from our marriage counselor, God bless his heart (and his patience). I have a theory as to why it's true. See if it makes sense to you: How many times have you heard of men hanging onto their old high school football jerseys for decades, or never wanting to replace that hideous lopsided, puffy recliner in the den, simply because it's his and has been his forever? It's comfortable. His stuff is broken in; he's used to it. It smells like him. It's worn in all the right places.

Do you know how many wives have told me that for decades, they've had to weed through their husbands' underwear and tee shirts and throw out the dingy, holey, stained ones with dry-rotted elastic? If we didn't weed out their old nasty drawers, they'd keep them and wear them forever. Men just look at life that way, hoping some things will never change and scratching their heads in frustration when they inevitably do.

It just makes sense, then, that they look at their wives that same way. When a man marries a woman, he truly believes she'll stay the same sweet, flirtatious, all-the-time-in-the-world-for-him girl she started out to be. When she changes (or "evolves," a term we'll examine in a moment) -- and she will -- he's confused, disappointed, and disillusioned.

The Catch-22 here is that it's just a woman's nature to evolve. Part of the reason for that is the fact that our lives do have such distinct phases with real and shifting demands.

For instance, there's a reason we often hear tales of a man feeling left out, becoming jealous even, when a new baby arrives. His wife's attention, heretofore enjoyed by him and him alone, is divided, and especially in the beginning, the baby gets the lion's share of it. The man is confused. Something's changed.

I've often wondered if husbands and new dads might be more understanding of the monumental changes -- evolutions -- a woman undergoes when she has a child if he could experience them himself, if even for a day. I have no doubt there would be big dollars thrown at medical research to make it all better if men could experience the joy of childbirth, nursing and healing for just a 24-hour period. I'm not one to bring hormones into the picture when examining female behavior (except as a last resort), but in this case, if the shoe fits...

Our hormones are going crazy after giving birth. Our bodies are doing their best to accommodate the new little one, while also trying to get back to a pre-pregnancy state, with little or no sleep. If we choose to breastfeed, we start carrying around two quarts of homogenized, all the time, in our sturdy utilitarian bras (the folks from the Spanish Inquisition still make them). We dispense that milk any time any baby cries, no matter whose baby it is. That alone comes with its own set of challenges. I couldn't go to Wal-Mart for months after giving birth to my son. I felt like a vending machine.

Our uterus is shrinking; our breasts are engorged. Our abdomens look like unbaked pizza dough. And our hips, well, they've been doing their own thing for more than nine months now, so why should that change?

We're tired, anxious and madly in love with this baby, yet this new little person terrifies us. Will he break? Will I lose him? Will I forget and leave him in the shopping cart? This tiny little precious life depends solely on us for survival; it's the biggest responsibility we'll ever assume. When our husband's pressing concern is how soon we'll be race-ready again for "going upstairs," that creates conflict in the marriage.

We change. He gets confused. Changing wasn't part of the bargain, in his mind. It's non-negotiable in ours. The addition of a child into a marriage is often the first, biggest test that union faces.

The flip side of that coin, of course, is the fact that men, as a rule, do not change. It isn't fair to a man either, when his wife gets frustrated that he's doing the very same thing(s) he's done for years, only now those things irritate her. They used to be endearing; now, they've become annoying. When it comes to men, we are learning in our thirties that what we saw at first is, as the saying goes, exactly what we got.

Jill, for years a stay-at-home mom before training to be a paralegal, has been married for forty-three years. She and her husband might just be one of the best-matched couples I've ever met. They truly love each other. They just fit, and when she shared with me that they came precariously close to divorce when she was thirty-six and he thirty-eight, I'll admit I was shocked. "What on earth happened?" I asked, as we each refilled our wine glasses and nibbled on some more cheese.

Her answer astounded me at first, then it made me laugh right along with the other women in our circle. "He cleaned his ears with his car keys," she answered with a straight face. "Every day, at least once a day, he'd clean his ears with the same key on his key ring, and it got to the point that I fantasized about just jabbing that key all the way into his ear the next time he did it."

I could not believe that this kind, gracious, unflappable mother of four had just told me she had thought about jabbing a key into the side of her husband's head at one point in their marriage. As she continued to tell me about the ear cleaning habit that almost cost her husband his very life, or at least nearly got him maimed, she laughingly added that the first time she had seen him do it was in high school, before they even started dating.

"Wait a minute," I asked. "You knew he did this before you married him? Before you even dated him?" She answered that yes, she did. It just so happened that while they were in their thirties (and about fifteen years into their marriage), one night after dinner while she was cleaning the kitchen and he watching the news and cleaning his ears, that the awful thought had occurred to her, out of the blue and very clearly. After that, when the idea would surface periodically, it didn't seem so awful any more. She was kind of getting used to the thought, actually visualizing how she'd do it if the time was just right. "Oh I loved him. I've always loved him," she answered when I put the question to her.

Of course, the moral to Jill's story is not that she and her husband nearly divorced or went to prison over a disgusting ear cleaning habit. It's simply that that one irritating habit had come to represent so many things over the years that she really believed would change, only because she wanted them to:

With respect to parenting, she was the disciplinarian; he was the good guy.

Every now and then, she wished fervently for the privilege of going into a bathroom alone, without an audience or an emergency requiring her attention, for just five minutes. That would of course require her husband running interference with the kids and the dogs, which never happened. Ever.

Anytime she asked that something be done around the house, that something was immediately dropped to the bottom of his honey-do list.

He always left his slippers on her side of the bed at night, a habit she never could figure out but that irritated her beyond measure.

He passed up a promotion at work because he didn't care for the man who would have been his new boss, even though the move would have meant more money that they sure could have used.

And the list went on. In other words, the stresses and pressures of life and the familiarity which they had with one another in their late thirties was just too much for her to handle for a brief time.

Then, she evolved.

She went back to school and still works today as a paralegal, loving every minute of it.

Her husband was confused as to why she might possibly want to go back to school when their youngest child had just started elementary school ("But you'll have all this free time. Why fill it up?"). In other words, "Why change?" She wanted to do it because she was evolving. She needed to change. After her first week of classes, the ear cleaning thing didn't bother her quite so much, which is a good thing, because he still does it to this day, presumably with the same key.

This story, which I still find pretty amusing, also illustrates something I've tried to teach our children. Love isn't an emotion or a feeling, at least when it brings a couple around to marriage. It is a commitment. It is the knowledge that we won't always have that fluttering in the pit of our stomachs at the mention of his name or the sound of his car in the driveway, coming to pick us up for our second date. It's the certainty that any marriage that has lasted for any length of time has seen its share of compromise, serving, consoling and yes, even tolerating. In our marriage, the only person more irritating than my husband can be, is me. I know that. He knows that. We love each other, and we both know without having to stop and think about it that we're in it for the long haul. As I said though, it took me a few tries to get it right. I'm not bragging; I'm simply observing and hopefully, I'm teaching our children in the bargain not to settle or compromise when selecting a life mate.

I have always told my girls that they'll know when they've met the man they want to marry when they can look at him and say, "I absolutely adore you. I respect you, and I trust you. And I know that one day, the way you chew, clean your ears (or insert another annoying habit here) and breathe will bother me (and the thought of jamming a key in your ear may surface momentarily), but I love you enough, anyway."

I suppose we can't thoroughly examine our thirties without talking about divorce, can we? Of course the D-word can strike at any post-marital age, but it makes sense to address it here, while we're exploring this phase of our lives. Divorce is an unpleasant fact of life, and statistics and trends differ depending on which data you may be reading. In my research, I found the data presented in so many different ways:

The National Center for Health Statistics reported the U.S. divorce rate for the 2001 calendar year was 47.6% of new marriages per capita. (per capita: 4.0 divorces / 8.4 new marriages = 47.6%)

Monthly Vital Statistics Report, Vol. 50, No. 14. (September 11, 2002). The 2004 report indicates a divorce rate of 50.6% of new marriages per capita. (per capita: 3.8 divorces / 7.5 new marriages = 50.6%) *Monthly Vital Statistics Report, Vol. 52, No. 22. (June 10, 2004).*

I found this information to be more boring than helpful. 3.8 divorces? 8.4 new marriages? What does that mean? So I kept digging, and I found this:

"Marriages are most susceptible to divorce in the early years of a marriage. After 5 years, approximately 10% of marriages are expected to end in divorce - another 10% (or 20% cumulatively) are divorced by about the tenth year after marriage. However, the 30% level is not reached until about the 18th year after marriage while the 40% level is only approached by the 50th year after marriage." *(a 1996 national study incorporating U.S. Census data)*

O.K. Now we're talking. Loosely translated, this information indicates that marriages are in the greatest peril during the first five years. Well of course they are, and for obvious reasons. Some couples simply wake up to the horror of having to compromise and live with a person that is not who they thought they were cracked up to be. The thinking goes something like this: "The problem has to be him, because I'm still the same awesome person I was when we got married." In other words, immaturity and unrealistic expectations are two sneaky culprits in young marriages. As an aside, I am not certain whether the common thirty-minute to three-day Hollywood marriages were factored in to this particular marriage statistic. I'd be curious to know.

The data also suggests that another 10 percent of couples will be divorced by the tenth year of marriage. As a marriage ages, so many other factors come into play. There's the always-popular mid-life crisis, a situation in which one or both parties tries to regain their lost youth by clutching shamelessly to a carefully manufactured illusion. In other words, no, that shoe-sized sports car and the adolescent, gum-popping girlfriend sitting beside you in it do not make you look younger. They make you look desperate, or kind of like her grandfather taking her out for ice cream.

Or, no. Those mini-skirts that reveal a bit too much, the painted-on, low-cut tops and the hanging-out-every-night-at-the-bar scene do not make you appear younger. It makes you appear sad and yes, desperate. At this stage, couples are stressed, they likely have children, they're becoming weary of life's demands, they may have sought escape in an affair; there are hundreds more reasons they throw their hands up and quit.

Other deteriorating factors creep into relationships, probably the most stealthy of which is sheer neglect and boredom. Sometimes, we simply suffocate our own marriages, killing them just like we would a neglected houseplant or pet. Marriage is hard work, its payoff riches beyond our wildest expectations.

Marriage is unbelievably tough, but very much worth the investment. I believe most women who have been married for a long time would agree with me on that one, I believe.

It's not until around year eighteen (give or take) of a marriage that the divorce rate hits thirty percent. If we can reasonably assume that a couple married at, say, age twenty-four, these numbers to which the data refers reflect what's happening in the lives of late-twenty-somethings to forty-somethings.

Of course, we can't ignore the fact that many women will stay by their husband's side no matter how many reasons there are not to. Maybe it's the peacemaker in those women, the do-gooder, the urge to hold the family together, the fear of being alone, the fear of not having enough money, or any combination of these specters that accounts for the phenomenon of staying in a marriage that is not healthy. Sometimes the wife will snap out of the trance, but sometimes they don't. A woman can and will endure pain, humiliation and unhappiness all in the name of keeping her family together. It's both admirable and tragic.

I will say from experience that, no matter when a marriage ends, it's not easy. It's not a happy occasion, especially when children are involved. And make no mistake, divorce is not the solution that many of us expected it to be; it simply serves up a different set of problems. It may be the lesser of two evils, but still – never easy.

I'm always amazed when I hear divorced couples say that their divorce was "amicable" and that they've remained friends. Really? Then why on earth did you divorce in the first place? What I hear about more often are the legal bloodbaths that so many of us have endured and participated in (no one is completely innocent, that much I know). Divorce changes us forever; it leaves yet another indelible mark, another scar.

The divorce itself is just the beginning of the new problems, especially if there are children. You and your ex-spouse's lives will forever be entwined, because you're linked together by those children. You two may hate each other with a scorching, blue-white passion, but you still have children to raise. As much as one of you may wish that the other would simply vanish from the face of the earth, your ex will not comply with that desire.

Think about it: school plays, birthday parties, graduations, weddings … the list never seems to end. Then of course, your grandchildren come along. Of course, many divorced couples have mellowed by that time, but many haven't.

I think two of the biggest hurdles in moving on with life after divorce are a) meeting and dealing with his inevitable new girlfriend, and b) starting to date again ourselves. In my case, I was very lucky. The two women I came to know as my ex-husband's girlfriends (one eventually became his wife) were actually very nice, very likable women. In fact, I like them a whole lot more than I do my ex-husband. That is not always the case in divorce, though. Often, the new girlfriend(s) bring a host of new problems with them in their cute little designer purses, paid for with money that should have been put toward tuition, braces or other such expenses. Many of the women with whom I chatted in researching this book had to deal with their ex-husbands' new twenty-something companions, and that included having to explain Daddy's apparent mid-life crisis to their children. Sometimes, these young women seemed to fit more appropriately in a kindergarten class – fingerpainting -- than in a relationship with the father of children only a few years younger than they. But we check them out and they us, sizing them up but more importantly, paying close attention to how they interact with and treat our children. In my book, if the new woman treated my children well, that was all with which I was concerned.

Then of course, we are faced with getting back out there and dating. It's been so long, and we are out of practice. Here again, if we have children, dating takes on a whole new importance. Yes, we want to be with an attractive man, an ambitious man who's still a family man, one who has all the items detailed on our checklists (which are somehow a lot longer now than they were the first time around). But now we are also dating on behalf of our children, always with them in mind. "Will they like him? Will he like them? Is he safe, kind, loving, attentive, good at middle school math…" The list goes on and on. It's exhausting. Let's get back to the lighter topic of the divorce itself.

There are the holidays and grandparent visits that have to be divided up fairly. When you think about it, divorce brings on more reasons to work together and get along than the marriage ever did. Such is the irony of life and pairing up, I suppose.

The good news that I kept gleaning from my research is that the divorce rate in the U.S. appears to be declining. Two factors are emerging as reasons for this trend: couples are waiting until later in life to marry (which I'm assuming means they're more mature from the get-go), and frankly, the ailing economy has more couples sticking it out for financial reasons.

Whatever our reasons for leaving a marriage, if that is in fact what we choose to do or it is a choice that was made for us, we women handle life after marriage in many different ways.

While we're on the subject of unpleasantries we encounter in our thirties, let's examine the health maintenance issues to which we must attend as thirty-somethings. Presumably, for about 10 years we've already been enduring that annual festivity known as the "female checkup," which of course includes the celebrated Pap smear and the delightfully fun mammogram. The first doctor who administered the Pap test to me had a picture of a big smiley face painted on the exam room ceiling, grinning down at

God knows how many uncomfortable women over the years with a knowing smirk on its face.

As if that test isn't bad enough, the surgeon general issued his recommendation to add an annual mammogram to the yearly humiliation. It's a recommendation I support 100 percent, by the way. Insurance companies, if you can imagine, are trying to backpedal on the importance of having the breast check done yearly but again, the dollar is the ultimate motivator for them. Let's hope they never get their way on this one.

The mammogram, I feel sure, was devised by a male doctor with the help of an insurance company or two and a couple of seventh-grade boys. It's as if these guys and the insurance companies put their heads together and asked, "What's the cheapest, most uncomfortable, most embarrassing way we can test all these ta-tas for cancer? Oh we know, let's smash them flat and shoot photos of them!" And that's what they do. Come to think of it, isn't that a man's dream job? The last time I had a mammogram, I asked the technician (a male, of course) if we could just mash my extra arm flesh in the metal press, smash it flat and take pictures of it. No one would be the wiser, and I'd take the secret to my grave if he agreed to do the same. He did not find the humor in that, at all. Since then, I simply get myself geared up for the annual screening by standing in front of my refrigerator and slamming my ta-tas in the doors over and over as hard as I can. You build up somewhat of a tolerance for the pain after a while.

And on that note – marriage, divorce, career, children, new girlfriends, smiley faces and mammograms, we'll step across the brink into our glorious forties.

Being Thirty and Fabulous...and Exhausted

BECOMING OUR BIGGEST ADVOCATE AND MOST DEVOUT FAN (OUR FORTIES)

"I am my own woman."
-Evita Peron

This decade, by far, so far, was hands-down my favorite, although the fifties are looking pretty good too. Is there anything more seasoned and self-assured than a woman who has been mellowed by marriage (and possibly by divorce), children, experience, patience, tenacity, heartbreak, hard work and reward? I can't imagine what it might be. A woman who knows herself and is comfortable with who she is, is a pure delight. One can almost bask in, and certainly take comfort in, her light. It's a beacon to younger women trying to juggle life and relationships.

It's been said that a woman in her forties can choose to fully bloom or silently stagnate at this stage. I don't think I really understood what that meant until I was actually in my forties, and the best way I can describe the new mindset that took up residence in my head at that age was just that: one of choice. It seems to be during this wonderful decade of a woman's life that she not only recognizes the fact that she can choose happiness, assertion, accomplishment, improved health or whatever else presents itself before her; in her forties, she actually makes those choices with her own well being in mind. Oh sure, her family and home and career are still vitally important but in her forties, a women wakes up to the fact that she's just as vitally important. In fact, she's very likely the linchpin that holds everything else in place. It's a wonderful, comforting, sometimes unfamiliar and exciting realization. As hard-wired caregivers, it's very likely that the last time we put ourselves first was way back in our teens, and who used that power for good during that stage of life? I certainly didn't.

The overwhelming majority of women (myself included) who have shared their personal experiences in this book have shared a similar self-awakening at this stage. What is it? Is it hormones? Experience? Wisdom? I don't know, but it was such a clearly marked mindset turnaround for me, I can almost describe it as a rebirth. Mind you, the self-awakening has nothing to do with selfishness; rather, it has everything to do with realizing and coming to terms with our own self worth, with having the chance to finally slow down long enough to get reacquainted with ourselves, with liking the woman we are and being excited about making choices to make her even better.

Earlier I mentioned that, by the time a woman steps into her forties, the business of living her life has likely mellowed her. You might raise your eyebrows at my use of the word "mellowed" with respect to marriage and children, and certainly with respect to divorce; some women might say that raising a family and being married has virtually sucked the life right out of them. And anyone who's endured the hell of a divorce can tell you that it's most often a brutal, gut-wrenching, stressful, no-holds-barred bash-a-thon, attorneys take all.

Women everywhere have said to me that at times, it seemed that their husbands and children did try to push them beyond their capacities to cope, beginning with those never-ending sleepless nights with infants to those, well, never-ending sleepless nights with teenagers. On particularly difficult days I used to imagine that, while my husband and children may not have been trying to kill me in the most literal sense, they were most definitely trying to wear me down and break me, maybe even drive me crazy. On some days, they came awfully close to succeeding.

But then come our forties, those glorious years packed into a decade that serves as the flipped switch and makes us stop and say, "Wait a minute. What about me?"

I really was almost forty years old before I learned that in order to continue to give and give, to keep pouring out into my family and career, I had to occasionally fill myself up again. I credit my husband with teaching me that; up until I met him, as a single mom I stayed on "autopilot: wide open" all day, every day. Being a single mom is both demanding and punishing. Leaving your children every day to work a full-time job to come home and start your second full-time job while juggling guilt, exhaustion and a nagging feeling that you're not doing any of it right, pretty much sums up "single mom." When I met my husband about 15 years ago, he gently and generously showed me that I needed to stop every now and then and take care of me by pampering myself. I was delightfully amazed to discover the he was right. I was, in fact, a better wife, mom and employee when I regularly set aside time – even a little – just for me.

Every woman takes care of herself, indulges herself, in her own way once she makes up her mind to do it. Some begin to frequent spas; others take up a sport they've been longing to try. Some women choose to go back to school, earning that postponed four-year degree or pursuing a graduate degree. Others begin to travel to destinations they've only dreamed of until now. Whether it's cooking classes, physical pampering, fresh mental stimulation, auto repair classes or a Pilates and Margaritas class (my own personal choice there for a while), women wake up to their own interests and passions in their forties, and I love it. We are rediscovering ourselves with a brand new pair of eyes and a galvanized heart. In other words, as our friend Benjamin Franklin observed about women so many years ago (at least I have heard this quote attributed to him, but I can't swear to it):

> *"At twenty years of age the will reigns;*
> *at thirty, the wit;*
> *and at forty, the judgment. "*

It's true anyway, no matter who said it.

I'll tell you something else that makes our forties spectacular, and that's a renewed appreciation of, a drawing nearer to, our friends. We may rekindle long-standing relationships when possible, and we find new women we'll come to treasure as close friends. There is strength, solace and sisterhood in a gathering of women, whether it's two of us or twenty. I believe that with all my heart, and I attribute what's left of the female part of my sanity to my women friends.

I remember my thirties as being a whirlwind of busy, a tornado in the middle of which I, my husband and our children would pass frequently on the way to school, church, work, football, cheering, gymnastics, softball, soccer or golf. There was no time for me to foster female friendships; the majority of my friends were the moms whose children played the same sports that mine happened to be playing during any given season. The other moms I knew were in the same situation. There simply was no time to be carved out for our own standalone friendships. Then something magical happens with our children around the time we're in our forties, and all kinds of time is freed up, seemingly overnight.

Our children become pre-teens, maybe teenagers. In the blink of an eye, we parents are demoted from our status as "centers of the universe" to "chauffeurs and ATMs." When you go from being someone's whole world to an inconvenient but necessary embarrassment, you suddenly find yourself with a lot more time on your hands. At first, I resisted this shift in my universe because you see, while I had always been the center of my children's lives, they had also most definitely been the center of mine. I simply couldn't understand why they would ask me to just drop them off at school or the mall or the movie theater, never actually driving past the group of kids they were meeting, nor kissing them, nor even waving goodbye. I was supposed to pretend as though I didn't know my own children? Yet I was also supposed to hand over dinner and movie money, maybe sweeten the pot with shopping money to boot? As you can plainly see here, I am still not over that phase of their development, and my youngest is well past it at nearly 21 years of age.

In hindsight, I get that this pulling away by our children is part of the natural progression of life and necessary to healthy development. Blah blah blah. I'm supposed to say that, I know, and I suppose it is true. When it first started happening, I didn't think I would survive it, but then something else equally as magical happened. I finally stopped puzzling over it and feeling sorry for myself, feeling almost as though I no longer had a purpose in life. I realized there was more time in my day that was not scheduled or otherwise spoken for. Yes, my husband and I had more time for each other, but I also had more time for me. That's a rare commodity for a mom, and one that's an awfully long time in coming. In truth, I had no idea what to do with all this new-found "me" time. Knit? Crochet? Not likely. I'm all thumbs, and patterns perplex me.

Gardening? Yes, I did pick that up. My dogs started getting a lot more of my attention, too. Looking back, I feel kind of sorry for them. I talked to them non-stop. I think it was too much pressure for them.

Sadly, as most of us have experienced first-hand, some old friendships don't survive the dry spell that is that time required to get our children to an age at which they're less dependent on us. Happily, some do. Social media sites have certainly made the reconnection process much easier, but we'll talk about those and technology in general in just a bit. I have to be in the right frame of mind to even approach all that business.

There's something so deep-down soul-satisfying about spending time with good women friends, isn't there? My circle of friends has always been small by design, and I suspect many women can say that same thing, as illustrated by the well-worn axiom:

> *"Men love little and often,*
> *women much and rarely."*
> *– Victor Hugo*
> *(French poet and novelist)*

This notion may not have been passed down from one woman to another in so many words; in fact, it's been more often passed down using no words at all, but rather through example and intuition.

Women have to feel a connection, a bond, with another woman in order to be the true friend and confidant she longs to be (and for whom the other woman longs, as well). We do not take genuine friendship lightly. We treasure it, preserve it, polish it as needed, nurse it when needed, and pack it away when needed, giving everything of ourselves because we want to, because we feel that it's healthy and it's reciprocated.

One of the groups of women with whom I spent time for the purpose of collecting Mama's advice (and also because I love them) met me at our favorite Italian restaurant around Christmas time last year. Although we all knew that we'd eventually get around to talking about the book and sharing family wisdoms, we talked about dozens of other things first. Our conversations always have a pattern, wide and circling at first, then more specific and detailed as time passes and we've all settled in.

I mused, as our conversation progressed, that there was a recurring theme that each of us touched on this particular chilly Atlanta afternoon. And then it hit me. I realized we had become that table of ladies other people listen to and laugh at. We each had our own aches and pains we addressed that day at lunch. For me, it was my hips. They ache, especially in cold weather. This started in my late forties. I am a side-sleeper (or I used to be), and one night I found that I just couldn't do it because the pressure made my hips hurt. They've hurt ever since. Now I am a back sleeper. That was a tough transition, let me tell you. You see, I was a stomach sleeper as a young woman. In my late forties, I got tired of being the only female in my family with no chest to speak of, so I paid a wonderful Atlanta cosmetic surgeon to fix that. Ever since, I've been too afraid of popping my investment for something as silly as maintaining my reputation for being a lifelong stomach sleeper. Anyway, now I am a vulnerable, exposed back sleeper. Let's hope nothing happens to prevent that; my only other option would be to hang from the ceiling. There are too many jokes in that instance to address here, so let's not.

I am not a wispy, small woman. I believe I mentioned earlier that I come from sturdy German stock; my skeleton weighs more than the entire average female, fully dressed, carrying a purse. In my forties, my already sluggish metabolism slowed pretty much to a crawl, then I'm convinced it stopped completely for a time. Exercise, I understood, was critical for me for that reason as well as all the other health benefits it offers. I have exercised faithfully for many years, and I think my hips are finally crying "Uncle. We can't take it any more." They really hurt when it gets cold, and I am sad to say, I can now predict oncoming rain or even elevated humidity with them. My ankles are a mess, and my knees have already started protesting loudly and often. One has recently been repaired; the outcome is still to be determined.

But back to our cozy little lunch. My friends each had their own woes to share: neck, shoulders, hands, feet, legs, and of course, the requisite laundry list of "female" ailments. It took at least an hour and two glasses of wine to just list, describe and compare our physical maladies.

This would probably be a good time to address the elephant in the room, so to speak, and that's the issue of how much harder it is to lose weight and maintain a healthy weight in our forties than it ever was before. Oh and what I mean when I say that is that it gets more difficult for women, not for men. I've been told the change is hormonal, of course. At any stage of a woman's life, what isn't?

Now I have struggled with my weight -- no lie -- since the day I was born. Rest assured, I'm not one of those women who swears she never eats a thing and still gains weight. I know women who eat like football players and are as thin as rails. It's one of life's cruel curve balls, but life's full of them.

I do eat. I enjoy food. I love the social rituals that involve beautifully prepared and well-presented food, good wine and designer cocktails, rituals which here in the South include everything from tee-ball games to weddings. In general though, I try to eat a well-balanced diet most of the time. I avoid fast food and soft drinks like the plague, and as I mentioned earlier, I exercise religiously.

You can understand, then, my sense of injustice and betrayal when, in our forties, my husband and I decided to get fitter, together. This was one of our "let's spend more time together" ideas once our children began spreading their teen wings. We hired a personal trainer, a bald, intimidating-looking former college wrestler without an ounce of fat on him, and with even less compassion. He worked both of us like yard dogs in the gym, and he also outlined nutritional plans for each of us to follow.

Right from the start of this cardio-driven endeavor, I felt cheated. My nutritional plan included about one-third the calories of my husband's. My list of food options was much shorter than his; the portions much smaller. For instance, my breakfast would consist of, say, a thimble full of bran cereal, half a grapefruit (one of the few fruits I absolutely detest), a tablespoon of unflavored Greek yogurt and 6 flax seeds. His breakfast included lean meat, eggs or egg whites, wheat toast, yogurt, milk, coffee and juice. I stuck rigidly to the confines of my plan and lost eight ounces in the first week. My husband stuck to his plan, plus he added birthday cake, beer and several trips through his favorite fast-food drive-thru restaurant on what he believed to be the sly. He lost eight pounds that first week. The following week, when we upped the intensity of our workouts, I actually gained two pounds. My husband was disappearing before my very eyes after just two weeks, and I was juggling the same few ounces, back and forth, off and on. After a month of that frustrating nonsense, I bowed out of the joint training/nutrition pact and decided to do my own thing.

Oh don't get me wrong; the trainer was top-notch and knew what he was doing. I'm just extremely competitive and a very poor loser. Although my husband and I had the same goal of fitness, I somehow felt that I was losing, that this venture was not fun at all, at least not for me. And I couldn't bear to see that look of combined pity and smug victory on my husband's face at every weigh-in (you know, that look that only your husband can muster that says, "well the important thing is that you tried, honey").

The fact of the matter is that it's when we're in our forties that many of us first start to feel a little wear and tear. Our faithful bodies (hopefully they've been faithful to us up to this point) are starting to ask us to slow down, just a bit. I refer to faithful bodies, but by this phase of life, some of us have already been terribly betrayed by them. I lost a dear friend to that shrewd, cunning monster -- cancer -- when we were both in our forties (she only forty-two). One day, she was fine, beautiful and alive, and the next she was terribly ill, but still beautiful and always so genuinely sweet. She maintained the most courageous attitude for the next year or so, while cancer spread and settled everywhere inside her, uninvited and voracious. Yes, our bodies can cruelly betray us no matter what safeguards we take. That fact makes itself known more and more often as we advance in age.

While I know cancer and other illnesses can strike anyone at any age, I do remember hearing of it among my friends and acquaintances more frequently, beginning in my forties. Of course, as we all age, the more often we hear of the deaths of our own friends, and of other people "our age." It's sobering. I think it's also the reason that many of us pay closer attention to our physical health during our forties if we haven't before. And when we suddenly find ourselves with more time to pursue our personal interests (because our kids don't want us around as much), that's the perfect opportunity to go out and find a gym, an exercise class or some other activity we enjoy enough to continue long-term.

Personally, I prefer to work out alone, as I just explained after the joint marital fitness venture with my husband crashed and burned. Well before the "couples training disaster" (as my husband and I refer to our failed fitness bonding attempt in order to fend off arguments), my first serious foray into organized exercise classes back in the 1980s was first jazzercise, then step aerobics. Both pursuits always looked like so much fun to me — a lot of work, but fun nonetheless. In my thirties, I actually began walking, then jogging with a neighbor, a girlfriend whose children were about the same ages as mine. We'd walk, talk and solve all the world's problems every evening after dinner. But my friend and walking buddy moved away, and I began feeling the need to try something new, to add to my bag of fitness tricks. Besides, I'm not built for jogging any more than a grand piano without wheels is built for roller skating.

Now every woman knows that, when we pick up a new form of exercise, the very first order of business is to go shopping. "You have to have the proper tools for the job," my dad used to say, and in my mind, exercise is no different from any other job. Remember what exercise garb looked like in the late 80s, early 90s? Oh yes I did; I ran out and bought several of those shiny, painted-on leotards with the high-cut legs (that should have only been worn by very, very thin women), a few pairs of blindingly unforgiving, shiny tights (yes, I even bought a tomato-red pair) and the proper shoes. I walked self-consciously in to the first class by myself, sure that all of the other women in there were professional dancers who had been wildly gyrating in perfect sync to the Go-Gos and the Bangles for years. As is customary with me, anytime I try something new that requires coordination and balance,

Becoming Our Biggest Advocate and Most Devout Fan (Our Forties)

I was nervous, as I have been gifted with neither. I crept to the safest spot I could find in the brightly-lit room, the very back corner and far away from the floor-to-ceiling mirrors. Looking around while trying to be inconspicuous about it, I saw that many of the women were stretching and jogging in place, mouth-breathing and psyching themselves up for what some might have mistaken for childbirth instead of a mere exercise class. I was already intimidated, instantly reminded of that scene in *Rocky* when Stallone finally reached the top of the steps, not the least bit winded.

I followed suit, stretching and jogging just enough to look engaged but not enough to hurt myself. Something popped when I bent over to touch my toes. I prayed it was a ligament or tendon or bone, not something critical like a seam in my tights. If my fat found even one tiny hole through which to escape, it would pop out like canned biscuit dough, and my cover would be blown before I ever got the chance to embarrass myself by actually dancing in some sort of attempted rhythm.

I won't drag this painful story out much longer, except to say that I was terribly uncoordinated and out of step the entire time, but I actually did fine and really enjoyed myself. I stuck with it and have since included cardio kickboxing, yoga and pilates in my constant quest for health and fitness. I wasn't kidding when I referred earlier to a "Pilates and Margaritas" class. I actually did that for a few months, just because the class was offered. Because I could.

One of my friends has been trying to convince me to try a belly-dancing class offered at our gym, but I just can't bring myself to do it. Nobody wants to see my belly, dancing (least of all me). Too, there is no telling what kind of damage I'd do to my back with all that gyrating and undulating. My knee? Forget it. There should be an age restriction in that class: No one under forty allowed. No, make that no one under thirty, and very well insured at that.

The bottom line here is that we women, we moms, have both the time and a renewed inclination to take care of ourselves during this phase of our lives. The irony is that at first, for myself anyway, the exercise brought on more aches and pains than I was used to. Still, it's necessary, critical, because it's in our forties that our risk of developing heart disease and other serious conditions begins to climb. There's really nothing funny to say about that, is there? I will just take this opportunity to share what most of us already know anyway; heart disease is the number one killer of women in the U.S., causing one in three deaths in women every year. About 42 million women are living with cardiovascular disease this very minute, many not even aware of the lurking danger. The symptoms of a heart attack in a woman can differ greatly from those in a man.

Education, exercise and a balanced diet, not diamonds, are a girl's best friend in the health department at this age and beyond. With that said, let's move on to another phenomenon no one warned me about that happens to us in our forties, and that's the appearance of random, unwanted facial hair.

There. I said it. I truly did not know that women could grow noticeable facial hair until I started seeing it on my friends which meant, of course, that they could see it on me as well. Oh I'm not talking about sporting a full beard or even a scruffy five-o'clock shadow, but if you're forty or older, you know exactly what I'm talking about; you can admit it. We're friends by now.

I was actually with one of my girlfriends when she first discovered her first sprout of facial hair, defiant, alone and obvious, on her chin. She was forty-two or forty-three at the time, I believe, about five years younger than I am. She and I were working out together at our gym, as we had for years. We were lifting weights and "watching our form" in the floor-to ceiling mirrors (those awful, truthful atrocities that only gyms, jazzercise class rooms and department store fitting rooms can get away with). Translated, that means that my friend and I were both probably just checking to see if our profiles were improving at all since we had started exercising together a few months earlier, and at the same time checking out the young trainer behind us doing leg presses. Not that we would have ever acted beyond a mere glance at the trainer, mind you. I am happily married to a man I lovingly refer to as Superman. Still, I liken the act of "looking" to staring at the beautiful cookies and cakes in the bakery window, but never actually tasting them. It's just fun to look every now and then, just to see how other men don't measure up to my cookie...er, husband.

Anyway, my friend and I had a bad habit of laughing and talking at the gym more than working and sweating, and this particular day was no different. She was curling some dumbbells and watching herself in the mirrors under that hideous lighting that seems to go hand-in-hand with floor-to-ceiling mirrors. All at once, in mid-sentence, her eyes widened and she exclaimed, "Oh my *God.* Why didn't you tell me that was there?" She was standing nose-to-nose with her reflection in the mirror, staring in horror at a hair that had grown to be about an inch long, sprouting defiantly from her chin. She looked at the offending new growth as if she had sprouted a third eyeball. She tilted her head this way and that way to see if there were any more whiskers.

Feeling her pain and empathizing (remember, being older, I've blazed this trail already), I convinced her that we should pack up our gym gear and hit our favorite coffee shop to commiserate, sort out this devastating new development so as to put it in perspective. We would simply drown our sorrows in a steaming latte.

I felt almost the same way I did before having "the talk" with each of my children, choosing my words carefully so as not to drive my friend screaming from the room. When we settled in with our favorite coffees in a quiet corner of the little shop, I laid out the facts for her, as plainly and as gently as I could. "I remember the first time I realized that something was happening with my hormones – either an increase in testosterone or a decrease in whichever hormone prevents us from growing a beard and mustache," I told her. Judging by the look on her face, my words were a bit too harsh.

I forged ahead, sharing my own discovery with her and trying to communicate how it made me feel at first. You see, when it happened to me, I was actually at my hair salon, my estrogen oasis, my refuge from the outside world, the one place on earth in which my friends and I can solve all the world's problems and figure out men in a neat, two-hour session. The salon's makeup artist was chatting with me while I waited for my stylist to finish working her magic with her previous appointment. The makeup lady actually offered me a free makeover and suggested a facial wax, to get rid of "all this" as she put it, brushing her hand along the side of my face. "All what?" I thought to myself, turning around to look in the mirror. Squinting and leaning forward (I'm blind without my glasses), I saw what she was talking about. There it was, very fine and very blonde, but it was there just the same. Fuzz. You know, like very fine carpet or those rugs everyone had in the 70s that had to be raked in order to look right. On my face! I suppose I just never noticed it, or maybe I assumed it had always been there because it crept in so slyly and silently. You can only see it in certain lighting. I take a bit of solace in that but no, it has not always been there. It was a gift from my fabulous forties.

I couldn't bring myself to wax my face though, and I'm still not sure why. Perhaps that would've meant admitting the hair was there in the first place. Perhaps I knew I'd be committing to a lifetime of maintaining yet another beauty regimen. Yes, I know how crazy that sounds.

Oh well, I shared my story with my friend, we had a good laugh about facing down yet another hormone-driven shakeup, and I suggested she get a couple of good pairs of tweezers and keep one with her at all times.

Oh well. I still say the good things about our forties far outweigh the bad. Something happens (maybe it happens when the facial hair shows up, who knows?) that makes us sit up and take notice. It makes us stand up for ourselves. It encourages us to say what's really on our minds rather than simply going along to get along. I personally found the brand new outspokenness to be very freeing. And tweezers are cheap. Not a bad trade, all things considered.

Many women who have shared with me for this book have similar stories and fond remembrances of the emotional freedom that their forties brought with them. Let me share one story with you that I particularly love, because the woman in the story is a very dear friend of mine. Her name is Melinda. Not really, but to protect her privacy, that's what we'll call her here.

For as long as I had known her, Melinda had been in a marriage that was oppressive, degrading and strangling. Even so, she always maintained such a sunny, bright outlook on life. I have always admired that about her. No matter her circumstances, she always has a smile on her face and a positive spin to share. She has a son who is my son's age, and we spent quite a bit of time together when the boys were little. We've remained good friends ever since, and that's been more than twenty years.

As is the case with so many couples after ten or so years of marriage, Melinda and her husband separated and eventually divorced. It's a long story, but the short version is that she had finally had her fill of his addictions, contemptuous treatment and philandering. She left him, and I couldn't believe it. I was so very proud of her. It's difficult to watch someone you love suffer abuse of any kind. As it turned out, we each helped the other through difficult divorces, for as the late Madeleine Albright said many years ago (and I still say today):

"There is a special place in hell for women who do not help other women."

For some reason, many women (myself included) actually believe for a while that divorce might make our ex-spouses easier to deal with. I'm not sure why we think that, but we tend to. I know Melinda did. Speaking for myself and from my own experience, I wanted to believe that with the toxic marriage no longer an issue, the children would naturally come first in any situation. That was not my experience, and it certainly was not Melinda's. Divorce, like financial issues, too often brings out the absolute worst in people.

At any rate, one day in the midst of Melinda's very nasty divorce, she learned of a horrifying, shockingly irresponsible incident in which her husband was completely negligent while their son was in his care. With an insatiable alcohol addiction, after consuming too much of it one afternoon, he drove to see his girlfriend with their son in the car. He had carelessly endangered both their son and heaven knows how many other drivers on the road that day. Who knows how many times that had happened in the past? That one selfish action was the proverbial straw that broke the camel's back.

Melinda snapped. I mean it. There's not another word for what happened to her that day. After all the years of abuse and humiliation her husband had put her through, it was when she learned that he had carelessly and selfishly endangered their son that Melinda finally stepped out of the fog that some call coping, others call tolerating.

As soon as she learned of her ex-husband's flagrant and irresponsible indiscretion, she drove to the golf course where she knew he was playing a round that day. And I don't mean she just drove up to the golf course and parked in the parking lot; she drove right up to the tee box on the 9th hole -- in her Chevrolet Suburban.

Shocked and stammering, her husband threatened. He cajoled. He calmly reasoned, as only abusers will do with their victims when trying to handle them. It wasn't working. She didn't budge. She stood her ground, and she turned up the volume. The Pro Shop manager, peeking out the window in utter disbelief, called the police because of all the ruckus. Country Clubbers enjoying a sunny lunch on the deck stood up and craned their necks to see what all the fuss was about. Somehow amid all the screaming and confusion, Melinda and her ex-husband both ended up back in the parking lot next to his beloved truck, where he made the mistake of minimizing the seriousness of his actions with their son by saying something condescending and demeaning to her. Melinda calmly got out of her vehicle, opened the back hatch and removed a tire iron. A collective gasp rolled through golfers and lunchers, much like "the wave" at a professional baseball game. Melinda calmly removed the tire iron, quietly closed the back hatch of her monstrous soccer mom vehicle, and proceeded to pound the hell out of his beloved truck, gouging holes in the body and smashing the windows and taillights with wild-eyed abandon. Every blow punctuated her message, each syllable of her opinion of him emphasized by the sickening crunch of metal and the muffled shattering and tinkling of safety glass. Her ex-husband saw in short order that he was not dealing with the sunny, pliable wife he had been able to degrade and wipe his feet on for 15 years; he was dealing with an entirely different animal. He retreated to the cab of his truck in cowardly fear, shrilly calling 9-1-1 again and demanding to know what the holdup was.

The cops had to pull my friend – all five feet and 100 lbs. of her - away from the now-aerated truck and secure her in the back seat of their cruiser while the matter got sorted out, a fact I feel sure her proper

Becoming Our Biggest Advocate and Most Devout Fan (Our Forties)

Southern mama has never been told. She'll never hear it from me, either.

Melinda and I had just celebrated her fortieth birthday just two weeks prior to this incident. Coincidence? I don't know, but I doubt it. Incidentally, that was the first and only time in my entire life that I bailed someone out of jail. It was both frightening and thrilling at the same time, probably because I was just so proud of my friend. We snapped a couple of photos of the inside of the jail and the arresting officer before scurrying out into the night air. She's an avid scrap booker.

Now I don't condone violence or "destruction of personal property," which I believe was the most serious charge on the document I was reading as I put up the money to spring my friend out of the slammer. I was glad to bail her out, because it was her I had come to get, not the zombie she had become over the years just to get through the days. We celebrated her emancipation (on several levels) afterward, and of course each of us took a cab back home after said celebration.

You see, for years so many of us women have never dared to rock the boat, have always been considerate of others and have been quietly unobtrusive. Maybe it's just that being all those things for forty years is too much; is there something magic about the age of forty that makes us say, "Enough"?

Maybe. Or maybe it's a combination of having had enough, being well-seasoned and again, those ever-reallocating hormones. Whatever the reason, I liked my forties. A lot.

Armed with a new-found sense of self assurance and a priceless knowledge of ourselves, women (reluctantly, in my case) wave goodbye to our forties and open the door wide to tell Fifty to wipe its feet, come on in and let's get to know each other.

Becoming Our Biggest Advocate and Most Devout Fan (Our Forties)

FINDING BALANCE, DISCOVERY AND MAKING PEACE WITH LIFE (OUR FIFTIES)

"I would rather trust a woman's instinct than a man's reason."
– Stanley Baldwin
(former British Prime Minister)

Fifty. The big 5-0. Talk about another milestone birthday, and it's one that's celebrated in the uncomfortable land of mammograms, and our new annual dates with colonoscopies and bone density scans. Our fifties are that far-off corner that many of us turn, around which our social lives become largely populated by doctor appointments and medical tests, but we'll get to all that in a minute.

I can honestly say that fifty was the first birthday that made me stop a minute and think about my age. Fifty. Half a century. I couldn't technically say I was middle-aged anymore unless I expected to live to be a miracle of modern science, a feature on Willard Scott's Smucker's jelly jar label. At fifty, we're more than likely on the downside half of our life expectancy. That, for me, was a very sobering thought. It's the kind of thought that gives one pause and makes one take inventory of one's life. I still can't say that this age bothered me because of vanity or fear; it simply made me take a hard, honest look at my accomplishments and choices up to this point. It made me look at what I still had left to achieve and the short time in which I had to achieve it. Where did the years go?

I suppose every woman at this stage of her life takes the same personal inventory at about the same time. "Have I come as far in my career as I had hoped? Did I make the right choices with respect to career and family? Did I make the right choice to forego a professional career and devote my life to raising children and making a home? What if I had married (fill in the blank here) instead of (fill in the blank here, too)? What if I had chosen to stay married rather than divorce? What if I had divorced him instead of hanging on to the marriage?" These are weighty matters, made even heavier because we're looking back on them and wondering, maybe second-guessing. As Katharine Graham, who led her family's newspaper The Washington Post for more than two decades, stated years ago:

> ***"So few grown women like their lives."***

I wonder if that's true. I really hope not. I will say that in my research, relaxed as it was, I found the opposite to be true of the vast majority of women with whom I spoke. Even those who are finding themselves in situations they never foresaw (and again, those women were by far the majority), I still sensed peace and good-natured contentedness; I sensed acceptance, but rarely bitterness or anger. I sensed that a woman's ability to change had once again helped these women curve to fit their lives.

Never one to play the role of the helpless victim, Katharine Hepburn had a healthy outlook when it came to figuring out what might be wrong with our lives and how to fix it:

"We are taught you must blame your father, your sisters, your brothers, the school, the teachers...but never blame yourself. It's never YOUR fault...but it's always your fault...because if you wanted change, you're the one who has got to change."

I happen to agree with the late, great, very wise Ms. Hepburn. Playing the victim never got any woman anywhere, except maybe stereotyped.

But before we delve into the meatier matters with respect to our fifties, I want to tackle one issue right out of the gate. It's one that I've found humorous for years now, and I have to share it and hopefully get you thinking about it, too.

According to the popular website jezebel.com, women in this country spend an approximate 7 billion dollars annually on beauty products. That number does not include beauty services (hair styling, waxing, mani-pedis, etc.), but just the products alone. We do this in our quest for endless youth and beauty, digging in our heels against the inevitable journey toward old age, or at least its appearance.

"Twenties-in-a-jar," that is what's peddled to us day in and day out on television, on billboards, in magazines and on the radio. Creams, potions, lotions, butters, capsules, gels, even contraptions that tap and massage problem areas, and deliver electric shock to others, are hawked to a female market ravenous for the promise of never-ending youthfulness. I know; I used to be one of the most avid consumers, a cosmetics marketer's dream. My friends tease me because of the assortment of creams, glosses and potions I've purchased, their primary purpose really to keep stuff from sagging or at least deflect attention away from it: stuff like eyelids, arms, chin, rear end. Those are pretty tall orders for a relatively tiny amount of cream in a jar, but I bought them anyway, ever the faithful believer.

However, fashion legend Coco Chanel looked at it this way:

"Nature gives you the face you have at twenty, but it's up to you to merit the face you have at fifty."

It took me a while to figure out what Ms. Chanel meant by this statement, but I believe she's telling us that the way we live our lives and of course care for ourselves have more to do with our faces at fifty than anything we can purchase in the cosmetics department of a high-end department store. Our life story is written on our faces, ladies.

Other areas of our bodies? I'm still not convinced that I have overturned every stone in my quest for 'uplifting." It's become quite a challenge and believe me, it's not because I want to look twenty when I'm in my fifties. I want to look fifty and healthy. I want it to be apparent that I matter enough to me to take care of myself.

It hardly seems fair to me at all, the difference between what happens to a woman's derriere at this age (a definite southward migration and loss of tone) and what happens to a man's (which is nothing).

Here's a great example of the lengths to which we'll go as women to defy gravity: I was shopping with a girlfriend last summer, and we had wandered into one of those delightful lotion/body spray/lip gloss/candle boutiques that always smells simply divine. Without fail, I leave those stores smelling like a cross between a bountiful fruit bowl and some sort of floral arrangement sprinkled with spices, because I can't resist sampling all the different scents. I'm so greased up that I shine and sparkle after visiting one of those stores.

Anyway, this same boutique offers a line of products designed to target under-eye circles and crepe paper skin and you guessed it: that evil, pesky nemesis, cellulite. To our delight, there were tubes of each miracle product with a red "TRY ME" sticker slapped on the front. Our pupils dilated; our pulses raced. We didn't hesitate one second.

I believe I mentioned that it was summertime, and wearing shorts, we both bent over right there in the middle of the store, in the mall, and smeared the potion in the cellulite "TRY ME" tube all over the backs of our legs, getting as much on our butt cheeks as we could without getting arrested, so blinded were we in our desire to find the holy grail of cellulite eradication. The instructions on the tube directed us to let the product dry completely, then wait to notice the astonishing, miraculous results in mere minutes. Thrilled, sure we had finally discovered the cure for the common cottage cheese thigh and cheek, we embarrassed ourselves even further by blowing on each other's backsides to speed up the drying process, a move that promptly got a sales girl's attention and a curt, "May I help you?"

My friend and I explained that we were just experimenting with the "TRY ME" tube of the amazing cellulite cream. We did this as we backed up to one of the store's mirrors and watched, waiting to witness a true miracle, the latest world wonder, the Fountain of Youth in a sampler tube at the mall. As we were backing up toward the mirror preparing to witness this wonder, we both noticed that our thighs and backsides were burning a little. The feeling was kind of a menthol, wintergreen-ish tingling sensation that wasn't at all unpleasant. The sales girl assured us not to worry about the burn, that the sensation was simply all the double-secret, patent-pending ingredients going to work on that pesky cellulite.

I'm sure I don't have to tell you how this experiment ended. Once the cream had dried, all it did was dehydrate into a shrunken gelatinous coating with a sticky consistency, thereby randomly tightening the skin on our thighs and rear ends in blotches. We looked like we had been partially wrapped in cellophane – not a flattering look at all and not at all like the twenty-something's cellulite-free legs and backside the marketing poster promised. We each examined the other's handiwork with dismay; we had not, in fact, uncovered a cellulite-erasing miracle. All we had discovered was a $56.00 disappointment in a snazzy-looking tube. We both left the store that day a little sadder, a little wiser, and a lot stickier.

I suppose the moral of that story is that, if it sounds too good to be true, it probably is. The humor that I find in this story and the hundreds of others I've heard on this same topic is this: women spend billions on similar products perhaps not necessarily in an attempt to stay young-looking, but in an attempt to age well, or at least to age better than we would without using the miracle products. The irony of that quest of course, is that men as a rule age pretty darn well with little to no assistance, don't you think? The gray at their temples makes them look distinguished, wise and sexy at the same time. Their wrinkles seem to come from tanning on cruise ships and golf courses, not from worry, stress, smart-mouthed teens or a breakdown of skin elasticity due to wear and tear and yes, hormones gone haywire.

The most men spend on beauty products, from what I've seen, is whatever shaving cream, deodorant and toothpaste cost. Oh sure, I've seen those lines of men's cosmetics in the department stores, but I can't recall ever seeing a man standing there at the counter purchasing them. I suppose they send their wives, secretaries or girlfriends to buy them. Oh well. Somebody buys them, I suppose, because they keep making them.

Another issue I find interesting and along those same lines is a recent surge in late-night advertising that I've noticed, encouraging female hormone replacement therapy – so we women can be more romantic and have more fun with our husbands or partners. Or maybe there hasn't really been a surge in such advertising; I've been waking up a lot in the middle of the night lately, and it takes me a while to go back to sleep. I'll turn the television on to keep from staring at the ceiling and making minutes feel like hours.

The advertising that's shown in the wee hours of the morning is a whole different ballgame than what's shown in primetime ladies, in case you haven't seen any of it yet. It's an underworld, a parallel universe centered around body image, hair replacement and sex (not any of my favorite topics in a discussion).

I've seen ads for male enhancement products: devices, pills, mini-vacuums, splints, lotions, rays, pixie dust, you name it. Come to think of it, this may be where men spend their vanity billions, not on beauty products. I have news for you men, and you may not like it. The stage of life in which a woman's stomach pooches out no matter how many crunches she does, she is drenched in sweat at random, she sprouts a mustache and sideburns, and her moods run hot and sometimes homicidal, plus the fact that we often see sex as something else to check off the daily checklist, may have a little something to do with the fact that you need male enhancement assistance. It's just part of the natural progression of life. A woman can separate "sex" and "love." We may love our partners deeply, but there are stages through which we travel during which sex really is something at which we have to work, because there's just too much other stuff on our minds, or it could be that all of our crucial body parts are not in top working order. That's just my two cents worth but frankly, it makes perfect sense to me and probably goes a long way toward explaining the attraction to women half your age.

Apparently, all this makes sense to marketers as well. Lately, I'm seeing ads for female hormone treatments that will improve our lives as well as his: we'll sleep better, we'll get rid of restless leg syndrome (does that really go hand-in-hand with menopause?), the night sweats will stop, the mustache will thin and eventually disappear, and the icing on the cake: we'll be more turned on, more "in the mood," more excited than ever to have sex (er, "go upstairs") with our husbands. In the commercials of course, the glowing woman just raves about the product and her newfound joy, and the husband sits knowingly satisfied beside her on the sofa, grinning like a Cheshire cat and watching the clock. Is it bedtime yet?

I don't think advertisers make it clear in these ads whether they're talking about a pill or cream or a complicated contraption, or perhaps a combination of all those. Maybe I'm just dense and uneducated in that department. My guess is, if the advertisers are smart they're actually talking about a once-a-week cleaning service and a photo of a man picking up his dirty laundry and placing it in the hamper, or maybe cooking dinner and giving the kids a bath. The results would be about the same for most women as any hormone cream or gadget; I know both would turn me on.

But back to Ms. Graham's grim observation about women and our lives, and how so few of us like them at this stage. I've referred often to the delightful conversations I've shared with so many women in preparing to write this book. I've also listened to some serious and very moving accounts of what can take place, really, at any phase of a woman's life, but very often it's right here, in our fifties, that we can hit some rocky roads and often need help to navigate them. In fact, the theme was so prevalent I asked another marriage and family counselor to explain it to me, and I'll try my best to explain it here.

The probability of a woman being treated for a mental or emotional breakdown (or a "nervous breakdown," as the condition was called back in the days of June Cleaver's reign) increases as she enters her late forties and fifties. That may sound like just plain old common sense to some of you and hogwash to others. Either way, in the conversation I had with this counselor, he said something to me that I found absolutely astounding. In fact, I had to ask him to repeat it, just to be sure I had heard him right.

He told me that in the vast majority of cases, when stress and anxiety are caused by marital issues, it is almost without fail the woman who will suffer the emotional breakdown. It's almost without fail that she will be hospitalized and/or medicated for having had a "nervous breakdown," not her husband. Now of course this assertion could be caused by any combination of reasons, but I have my own theory, and the stories women have shared with me here bear it out.

Women intuit. We feel. By that, I mean to say that a woman perceives and senses, as much as she hears and experiences. A woman's intuition is very real, not a fabled knack or a hormonal quirk. We have to *feel* that our marriage is solid; we have to *feel* that our children are happy, that we are succeeding at whatever we do. You can tell us these things are true all day long, but until we *feel* that they are true, we are on shaky ground. Our world is askew. We have to feel it for ourselves to know it's true.

Does that make us crazy? Quite the opposite. But it does make us vulnerable. I loathe that word as it applies to women, but let's face it; it's the only one that fits. We feel so much and so deeply that we are greatly affected by those around us, particularly by those whom we love. If enough upheaval and discord occurs in our lives, especially during phases of change (such as becoming empty nesters, for example), the result can be anything from a brief hospitalization to a handy little prescription for anti-anxiety or anti-depression medication – often referred to as "mommy's little helpers" back in the 70s and 80s. Even women who have never struggled with either condition can be blindsided, especially during our fifties, with all its harmless-looking turbulence.

On the topic of becoming empty-nesters, this same counselor told me that, believe it or not, the empty-nester event is one of the most stressful in a couple's life and not surprisingly, so much more so in a mother's life. I would have doubted his word on that had I not experienced it for myself a couple of years ago. I know it sounds strange; it seemed that for years (especially throughout our children's teen years), the prospect of having an empty nest someday was all that kept me going. It's what got me through the sometimes hell that is known as parenting a teenager -- kind of a mom's optimistic spin on "this too shall pass." I imagined the empty nest phase of our lives to be filled with satisfying hobbies, exotic travel, new opportunities to date my husband, gardening, a more relaxed work schedule, and just a general feeling of accomplishment, peace and satisfaction. The reality was a bit different. First, I desperately missed having our house full of children. Yes, they left one at a time but even when we were down to just our youngest daughter living at home, there were always a lot of other kids around, too. They travel and hang in packs, you know. My withdrawal from our youngest began back when she was a senior in high school, well before we packed her off to college. With every college application and campus visit, the knife turned a bit more. The dread inside me grew. Poor kid. I know I drove her crazy. I'd cry on the way to campus visits. I'd cry when we completed the applications. I'd cry every time her high school hosted an event honoring that year's seniors. I suppose every woman handles her children leaving home differently. My older sister would tell me with excitement and conviction, "Well of course you'll miss them. But about fifteen minutes after the last one's gone, you'll love it." I can definitely say I took becoming an empty nester a bit harder than she did.

Luckily, my career actually demanded more of my time when our children had all left home. In my line of work, that's a blessing; it's just not what I had envisioned. There are times that I'm so busy that I'm not home for days at a time. When you're a writer, travel and media and book signings are blessings but alas, I'm also a creature of routine and habit. I get all out of sorts when I'm away from home for too long. I think that may be one of those things that comes with age but at any rate, here I am. I love what I do, so I comply with all that's necessary to do it.

When I am home, I talk to my three dogs all the time. I live in suburban Atlanta in a house that has white carpet, and I have three dogs - a fact that all by itself makes me a weirdo. I have in-depth conversations with my dogs. I run ideas past them. I praise how smart they are and lecture about the consequences of chewing things that don't belong to them. I share the latest dish about the neighbors and politics with them. They just look at me lovingly and wag their tails, which come to think of it was really all I asked of my teenagers when they were home.

So yes, being left all alone in a house that suddenly seems too big and too quiet can be quite a shock. It gives us time to think more about things that we may have been sweeping under the rug for decades, whatever they may be. It gives us time to partake in that horrid pastime known as self-examination. Add to that shock that no, you're not actually alone, you're likely there with your husband, a man whom you've passed briefly in the previous 18 years while heading to some sort of practice or other kid-driven event. You know, you can love a man based on the life you've built together and still not know how to be alone with him after years of raising a family. Here's why I think that's true: Children, once we have them, become our lives. They become the topics of our conversations. They become our hopes and our fears. They become our weekend plans; their friends' parents become our friends. And on the day that our children leave home (which in hindsight feels like about 15 minutes after they're born), we stand there looking at our husbands as if to say, "Who are you?"

Oh sure, there are couples who prepared for this time of life but I suspect that, more often than not, couples react just like my husband and I did, not prepared at all for this sudden onslaught of quiet, one-on-one time. We love each other. We have raised four children to be amazing, responsible young people, each of them with their feet set on good paths of their own choosing. But my husband and I didn't really know what to do with each other, how to spend our time (if not in a school or a school gym or on a ball field), how to go in a new direction without herding four children ahead of us. We're still figuring it out but let me tell you, it hasn't been easy. We're starting to get the hang of it. The payoff will be amazing, though. Of that much I feel sure.

I think the dichotomy with which I struggle on nearly a daily basis is the difference between how I feel mentally at age 51 and the way I feel physically at this age. I suppose I'd be remiss in not addressing this contrast with stark honesty. In my mind I'm oh, I'd say, about 25 years old. I feel joy and happiness and fear and irritation and excitement, just as I did 25 years ago. There are times that I feel incredibly sexy, times I feel pretty, times I feel fabulous, and then there are times I feel like a chunky, aging slob (I'm just being honest). I have a hard time reconciling my youthful mental state with my body's creeping, creaking betrayal.

My knees sound like corn popping when I walk up or down a flight of stairs; I recently had a knee surgery that provides me daily with bona fide verification that some of my important parts are wearing out. I have to wear special, homely-looking shoes because my paper-flat feet have finally gone on strike after half a century. Believe it or not, my wrists and hands have to be positioned just so in order for me to type pain-free, and typing is of course critical to a writer. I have a special keyboard that looks like something one might buy in a pornography shop. "Ergonomic," I believe it's called. I actually see a chiropractor weekly so that he can keep my hands, shoulders and neck in good working order so that I can continue writing. And recently, I underwent the newest and least invasive procedure for a total hysterectomy, which I'm sure will bring many new physical experiences and emotional challenges for both my husband and me. We're both really looking forward to that.

Let's not forget menopause and its harbinger, peri-menopause. Hormonally, where do I begin? If I'm not sweating, I'm crying. Or being irritated. Or thinking of taking flying lessons. Or scrubbing baseboards with a cotton swab (O.K. I was just trying to make a point. I've never actually done that with cotton swabs or baseboards). I imagine that sometimes, living with me must be like living with Sybil or a giddy, sobbing circus clown. This might be a good time to apologize to my husband - just a general, blanket, all-inclusive "I'm sorry, honey."

I've asked women to describe for me, in their own words, what a hot flash feels like. It almost defies description, doesn't it? I've had women say that it feels as though a furnace fires up inside, at their very core, and the heat radiates outward until you break out into a sweat and you're seriously considering stripping down to your designer skivvies, no matter where you are. Other women have said they begin to feel flushed, starting at their toes and ending with their hair. Still others tell me that it feels like having hot chills, whatever those are. Even at age 51, I've only experienced one (I think it was one, and it happened four or five years ago). I was sitting in a high school gym, watching my youngest daughter cheer at a basketball game, and I thought I was going to have to run outside in the January air, find a swimming pool, pull off all my clothes and take a dip in the water. It was that bad. Then again, the gym was packed, the athletes were sweating, our team was behind, and I tend to be hot natured, so who knows?

At 51, teetering precariously on the edge of menopause (so I'm told), my epidermis has retained just enough elasticity to jiggle when I breathe. The skin under my eyes looks like a crepe paper art project. My former dimples have actually become the parentheses we hear so much about in anti-aging skin cream commercials. Still, I like my face. I think Ms. Chanel would approve of it; it tells a story, and a good one at that. A happy one, for the most part.

I suppose this is as good a time as any to talk a little more in depth about hysterectomies, hormones, perilous mood swings and such. By the time we reach our fifties, we're going to face some or all of them by naturally aging or by undergoing surgery. A good many of the age-fifty-something women who have shared with me for the purposes of writing this book have had to undergo complete or partial hysterectomies, either for health or for quality-of-life issues. Even if the woman didn't have much choice in the matter, deciding to go ahead with a hysterectomy is a tough decision. I've always heard of women feeling nervous about removing the internal "mechanics" of being female, and I have to confess that for years, I thought that notion was silly. I mean, a woman is a woman, right? Whether she has all or some of the essential working parts that women have, a woman is, in essence, still a woman. However, now that I too have just had this gender-nudging surgery, I'll admit that I feel almost … sad? Yes, I think that's it. I feel sad, because this procedure most definitely draws a defining line in my life, a line between the me that could bear children (scientifically, anyway) and the new me, who can't. Even though I had no plans at all, ever again, to have another child, there's just something very final about what's no longer physically possible for me. It's comforting to know that I'm not alone in mourning the loss of those mysterious internal workings that govern the rhythmic business of being female. Then again there's always comfort in numbers, isn't there?

Oh yes, I have joked with my gynecologist and my girlfriends about the whole ordeal, because joking is what I do best when I'm nervous or anxious about something. I have joked about the possibility of growing facial hair (O.K. more facial hair) now that I've had the surgery. I have joked about having wild, neck-injuring, roller-coaster mood swings and whether I (and my husband) will need medication to cope with them. I really am serious; I didn't know whether I'd come out of surgery with my head spinning like Linda Blair in *The Exorcist*, or all Zen, calm and wise, like the gracious Oprah Winfrey.

I have joked about how much the organs to be removed actually weigh, so I can go ahead and log the weight loss in my journal. Is that being too graphic? Sorry. I suppose I'm still a bit anxious, so the jokes continue to flow, so to speak, however corny they may be.

In truth, I'm nervous and more than a little melancholy about the effects of the surgery and the fact that I was thrown head-first into menopause as soon as the procedure was over. My doctor, a delightful, tiny whirlwind of a bluntly honest woman, had already forewarned me. She said I might breeze through the onset of menopause just like my sister did, or I might start sweating and mood swinging while I'm still in the recovery room. I am right now dealing with the emotions and apprehensions that millions of women who are facing or actually entering the dreaded "Meno-monster" are feeling.

Menopause is that hulking, faceless behemoth that begins stalking women as soon as they first become fertile young girls, although they don't know yet that they're being stalked. Oh yes my friends, there most certainly is a biological clock, and menopause is straight-up midnight. Does that sound a bit melodramatic? Must be my hormones.

Is it hot in here?

But enough about my surgically-induced change of life. Let's get back to battling the signs of aging, a favorite pastime of millions of us girly-girls. The battle heats up when menopause descends upon us. Our skin becomes drier and loses some of its elasticity. Our hair can thin and become brittle. I take all of these symptoms as further evidence of how very angry God was with Eve when she committed her transgression in the Garden. The hits just keep on coming, and I'll just say right here and now that I'm very thankful for medical and cosmetic advances in dealing with all this upheaval and nonsense.

With respect to the issue of skin elasticity, one of my girlfriends almost talked me into getting botulism (Botox is the patented name, I believe) injections with her a couple of months ago. I still can't wrap my head around the concept of intentionally shooting a toxin into my skin that, if swallowed, causes vomiting and diarrhea, but I did go with her to get hers done. She gets the treatments like clockwork, never misses an appointment.

My friend is recently divorced and is having everything – and I mean everything – stitched, tucked, yanked, lifted, extruded or injected. I say "power to her," if that makes her feel good about herself. I am too much of a chicken to volunteer for any kind of injection not intended to save my life on the spot, but I applaud her and her right to get them.

As I said, I accompanied her to her injection appointment, surprised at the number of both men and women in the clinic's large waiting room. While I looked away during the procedure itself (she talked me into going back to the examination room with her, as if that would change my mind about the whole thing), I couldn't help staring at her that afternoon and in the days that followed. The effect of the botulism injection, coupled with the collagen injections she had gotten in her lips just weeks earlier, had an alarming effect. My friend, who's a stunning natural beauty anyway, looked perpetually surprised, with an expression much like a bass might have upon realizing it swallowed not just a worm but a rusty hook, as well.

I say all this with the utmost love and respect for my dear friend. I also obtained her permission to share those details, as my mama did not raise a fool. You see, my friend's husband left her several years ago for his secretary, who is literally half his age (cliché, I know, but true). Of course, the secretary was just a bit older than the three children whom he left my friend to raise, essentially, alone. Not long after the divorce was final, my heartbroken friend began scheduling cosmetic procedures left and right. She had her breasts enhanced and lifted (three kids, remember?), her chin sculpted and tightened, her face tweaked and her derriere plumped up. She even had her calves done. I finally asked her one day, while we were driving to get yet another procedure performed, why she was putting herself through all this pain and misery. Was she was getting all this work done to make herself more attractive to other men? She thought about my question for a minute before she answered.

"No," she said. "I do it to make myself more attractive to me."

I liked that answer. I thought that it was cuttingly honest, and I respect her for giving it. Nowadays, my friend is more at ease with herself and truly loving her life. She dates, but not too seriously. She has stopped getting all the surgeries (though as I said earlier, she still gets injected every now and then). I think it's possible that she simply ran out of things upon which to improve. We can laugh at the fact that, undressed, she looks like a well-constructed quilt, because every one of those scars took her one step closer to healing from one of the cruelest slaps in the face a woman can suffer: her husband tossing her aside for a younger woman because HE fears aging.

Whew. Is it hot in here?

I suppose another topic I'd be remiss in skipping while we're on the subject of our fifties is grandchildren, or as I like to call them, "God's ultimate do-over." My husband and I have looked forward to having grandchildren (when the time is right, of course) for years. We love our children passionately, and I think we did a pretty good job of raising them, but who doesn't look back and wish they had done a few things differently, done some things better? Enter grandchildren, rumored to be the most perfect, precious little beings ever created. I can imagine how terrific it will be to have them, because I'm relaxed enough now about certain things to enjoy them. Our friends tell us that having grandchildren is wonderful.

When my children were little, I remember being uptight about everything, all the time. I wanted them clean, healthy, well-dressed, well-behaved, respectful, and as athletically and academically accomplished as they could possibly be. In other words, I set myself up for needless disappointment, because nobody's child is perfect. I was and still am today living proof that no parent is perfect. I want to be, but I fall dreadfully short of that mark.

The other result of this perpetual uptightness is the fact that I know I missed out on the full joy of being with my children, of just *being* with them, when they were younger. I often missed the joy and amazement of watching them, learning them and yes, even learning from them. I wish I had gotten down in the dirt and just played with them more often than I did. I wish I had been sillier. I think a lot of us re-think our own parenting, do some armchair quarterbacking, but we do it because all we want is to be good and responsible mothers, who love our children and whose children love us. We want to leave a good and indelible mark on our children's lives.

If I had it to do over again, I can say without reservation that I'd wipe, wash and disinfect less. I'd work less. I'd tolerate less unhappiness (in other words, I would have divorced their father years earlier than I did). I'd most definitely laugh, goof around and hug more.

No, my husband and I don't have any grandchildren yet, but I can only imagine what a joy they will be. I've had women describe them to me as "perfection perfected," "blessings," and "sweet angels." They've told me that they get it this time around, that they do take the time to enjoy their grandbabies with wonderful abandon. They tell me that they see their children in their grandchildren, and that their love and adoration are doubled as a result. I can't wait until our children are ready to bring their children into this world. I can't wait to get my Grandma on.

And ah yes, we can't thoroughly address the topic of parents and parenting without talking about our own parents aging. It's right about now, in our fifties, that many of us find ourselves in the position of having to take care of our parents. We find the tables turned and our parents now being the ones needing care. My father, bless his heart, is still living at 93 years old. Over the past, say, ten years, my siblings and I have had to face some tough realities. You see, when a parent begins losing the ability to care for himself, to make his own decisions, it's not always immediately apparent to his children. It's almost certainly not apparent to the parent. It takes time, and sometimes it takes repeated incidents of the elderly parent doing things such as falling, eating poorly, getting lost, forgetting and the like to adjust, maybe even force, their children's perception.

In my dad's case, he had taken a couple of bad falls in his late eighties. He was also eating food that had well passed its expiration date, and he had lost the ability to keep up with his complicated regimen of daily medications. When a chronic illness landed him in the hospital several times in the same year, it was time for us to face some sobering realities. It was time for us to take care of Dad. Two of us were still raising young children, working and trying to keep spinning all the plates without letting any fall to the floor and crash. It became evident very quickly why ours is the first to be known as the "sandwich generation."

It's a strange feeling to be in the position of parenting your parent. It just doesn't feel natural. Perhaps that's why it takes us so long to realize it, to recognize the signs of our parents needing care. I know that in my father's case, we felt as though we were prying his fingers away from every vestige of independence he had ever known. He had to move from his house to a retirement community, because it just wasn't safe for him to live alone after a certain age. Yes, my husband and I tried having him live in our home with us, while our youngest two children were still in high school. Having lived alone for about twenty years before moving in with us, Dad just couldn't wrap his head around the fact that he really shouldn't walk around in front of our children and their friends in his underwear. Even when I tried talking with him about why doing such a thing was inappropriate and uncomfortable, he'd answer me with, "Well, I've done it for all these years, so why do I have to stop it now?" Sometimes, it really did feel as though we were trying to reason with a child. Incidentally, Dad only lived with us for a little more than six weeks. It just didn't work, he had simply done things his way for too long to try to mesh with our lives and where we were in them. It was too stressful on everyone, Dad included. He moved into a senior community after living with us.

We had to convince him to sell his prized possession, his boat, at about the same time he sold his house. Although he hadn't used it in years, he loved boating and the fishing that went with it for decades. His sight had begun to fail him, and it became necessary to tell him that he could no longer drive his car safely. That was tough for him. Every time we had to deal with another of his freedoms being lost, we saw the pain and resistance in his face. It was heartbreaking at times. It was the reality of parenting a parent.

Therein lies another stressor that rears its frightful head at about this time in our lives. We feel pulled in many different directions, financially, emotionally and with respect to our time. As women, as nurturers and natural caregivers, it's important to us to know – to *feel* – that everyone we love is getting what they need from us. It's utterly exhausting.

I had the opportunity to speak with a lovely woman named Arete, whose mother lived in the same retirement community as my father did until she was diagnosed with early stage Alzheimer's disease a couple of years ago. Arete's family is Greek – a big, boisterous, loving family who spent time with their aging mother every chance they got, bringing children and grandchildren to the retirement home right along with them. The sight and sounds of the entire clan were always happy ones to me.

The last time I saw Arete and her family was on a Sunday afternoon almost two years ago, and it was evident right away that something was amiss. The family's usually bright mood was somber; the conversation was hushed. When she and I spoke that afternoon, Arete confided in me that her mother, just that week, had received the frightening diagnosis of having early-onset stage Alzheimer's disease. Life would be changing drastically for this lovely family; the question of whether to send the grandmother to live in a facility dedicated to the care of Alzheimer's patients was not even being considered. The decision had been made that the sweet grandmother would live with Arete and her family.

I have not seen anyone from the family since that Sunday afternoon, but they have been in my thoughts often. I have several friends who are not only in the position of taking care of their parents; they are living the painful nightmare of caring for a parent who no longer knows his own children. They are living with a mom who does not know where she is or why she feels like a stranger everywhere she goes, so she cries all day and throughout the night. They are living with locks on windows and doors and the constant fear of their beloved mother or father wandering away, getting lost or worse.

One of the women I interviewed actually endures the pain of visiting both of her parents in an Alzheimer's-focused nursing home. Her mother and father do not know one another; sadly, her father has a "girlfriend" in that same facility, as he has no idea that he is married or to whom. The couple walk the halls together, holding hands and talking sweetly to one another, having no idea who the daughter or the mother is in the overall picture. It's a painful nightmare for this woman that plays out again and again, every time she visits her lost parents. Still, she visits every Sunday. A woman's love is a sturdy, enduring thing.

Patsy, a 56-year-old woman who spent a couple of precious, quiet hours with me talking about this very thing, confided to me that, while she could never consider placing her mother in a "home" for Alzheimer's patients, she dreaded the sound of her mother stirring every morning. Her stomach knotted with the halting, shuffling sound of her mother's too-light footsteps and walker coming down the hallway to begin another day. Patsy broke down and cried during our conversation more than once, ashamed for having these feelings, and my heart broke for her and for her mother. The emotional toll, along with the financial burden of hiring a part-time caregiver just so Patsy could tend to her home, family and medical billing job, were nearly unbearable. Often, they were unbearable.

The sad reality is that, when a parent's mind is scrambled by this insidious disease, their body seems to remain strangely healthy in contrast. This paradox cruelly prolongs the horror of Alzheimer's disease, and Alzheimer's in turn has changed the landscape of couples who likely had retirement, travel, a second career or anything besides this cruel, relentless reality in their future. More than one woman has wondered aloud in our conversations whether medical science has benefitted us or cost us with respect to aging.

Finding Balance, Discovery and Making Peace with Life (Our Fifties)

As a side note, it's worthwhile to note that while women are still more likely to be caregivers, the number of men caring for loved ones with Alzheimer's (or dementia) has soared from nineteen percent to forty percent in the past fifteen years (this according to the Alzheimer's Association). Families are being forever changed, and though the trend appears to be that the grueling burden of primary caregiver may be shifting to a more equal balance between men and women, the toll on families is still tremendous. In our fifties, unless we have already lost our parents, their care will move to a spot near the top of our list of things with which we must deal. The irony, of course, is that many of us are also starting to clunk and sputter physically ourselves.

Yes, women of our generation, I believe, are more fitness savvy. We understand the short- and long-term value of keeping our bodies fit. Still, with a half century or more of time and mileage on our bodies, stuff starts to happen.

I am fifty-one years old. Just a bit over a year into this decade, I've undergone one knee surgery and a hysterectomy this year alone. We still have children in college. My father is 93; my husband's mother is 78. Things are heating up around here – how to juggle it all? Thankfully, we have patience and wisdom in measures we've never known up to this point, taught to us by life and its experiences. I like who I am right now. The women I interviewed for this book who are in their fifties like themselves right now, I believe without exception. That's a good thing, because these are times during which we are taxed nearly beyond our limits.

I will say that while my husband and I thought life's everyday race would begin to slow when we hit our fifties, quite the opposite has been true, and that's O.K. Even though we rarely feel as though we're the ones steering the bus even now, the ride is never boring. We've learned by now that we're stronger and more resilient than we thought. Our children (especially our daughters) have come to understand that we were not trying to ruin their lives just a few short years ago. They get that we love them unconditionally, that we always had their best interests at the forefront of whatever we did, and that we can now be friends on a more equal plane. As they have gotten older, we have somehow gotten smarter, in every area but one that is - technology. I can't talk about being a 50-something-year-old woman, in the year 2012, without talking about my arch enemy, my nemesis: technology.

Even though I didn't want any of them, I have a smart phone, a racy, sleek little laptop, and a tiny little device that holds more songs than I've heard in my entire lifetime. Can anyone actually name six thousand songs, much less like and listen to that many? My car talks to me without my initiating the conversation, and it answers my phone without asking me whether I want it to. It tells me of impending danger up ahead; it alerts me when I cross state lines. It still startles me, and I've had the car for more than a year.

You see, I am a member of the generation that fell between the cracks, electronically speaking anyway. The generation that came before us didn't need to know anything about computers and such, and the generation that came along after understands these devices just as thoroughly and naturally as they know how to walk and talk.

Oh, some of us catch on. My husband is an electronics geek, a techie wiz. For that matter, my dad was until his eyes betrayed him by fading. I am not. I don't want to be. I am being dragged into this automated era kicking and screaming and clutching my big 1980s car-mounted phone that looks like a shoe box with an antenna. My new phone, which is about the size of a credit card, tells me what to do, and when. My electronic calendar is shared with everyone involved in my professional life, so new instructions are popping up on the phone's screen all the time. I feel like one of the tiny little metal balls that lives in a pinball machine, bouncing off this task and that, rambling around aimlessly, awaiting further instructions. My e-mails follow me, constantly distracting me from whatever I'm doing at the time, as they arrive with an insistent "beep."

I don't function well in a world driven by devices that beep, honk, talk, remind, buzz and demand. It's maddening to a person like me, but I'm told by everyone that I have to keep up with the times. Not many things make me feel dumb or inadequate, but technology and all that goes with it are the exception. I just don't get any of it. I like my paper and pen. I miss a typewriter. Do they still even make White-Out? I remember thinking what a head-spinning technological advance that thick, white, gooey stuff was to a wordsmith like myself. Now, I can change a sentence, eliminate a paragraph, or move around entire pages without having to re-type anything. That part is cool, I suppose, but I'd still go back to the old way of doing things if I had my choice. I'm very resistant to change (a lot of women are, as I learned when doing the research for this book), but I think I may take it to the extreme. "NID" my friend Michelle calls my condition: Not Into Details. She says it comes with the territory of being a creative type person.

Oh well, resiliency and patience – those are the two key traits that have gotten us to where we are in our fifties without losing our mind – or without losing most of it, anyway. At this age, we can look back with pride, regret, contentedness and maybe a little bit of longing for the days when our children were little. Oh, what would we do differently?

Finding Balance, Discovery and Making Peace with Life (Our Fifties)

But we can also look ahead and build on that wonderful realization that hit us in our forties (We matter! We have interests! We now have time to explore them!) And if we're lucky, we still have our life partner to walk through our fifties and into our sixties with us, holding our hands and whispering sweet encouragements from time to time.

ENTERING OUR SIXTIES

"Getting old ain't for sissies."
- Bette Davis
(American actress)

This is the first phase of life that I've written about in this book but have not yet experienced, so I've relied heavily on the priceless anecdotes of the women with whom I've talked who are in their sixties. These women have been gracious, open and honest, traits which seem to come easily at this stage of the game. I think, though, that the strength and self-assuredness I saw in these women, without exception, are by far my favorite qualities that sixty-year-old women demonstrate. Their strength gives me encouragement, something for which to strive, because I'm right behind them.

In my mind, up until I wrote this book, "sixty" was really the first age that sounded "senior" to me. Grandmas are sixty. Senior citizens are sixty. However, after talking with women this age and seeing firsthand this aura of strength which I so admire, I decided to do a little digging. I wanted to know more because, surprisingly, these women seemed to really like their age and where they are in life. Most have endured great hardship at some point or another, either losing a husband or even a child, but all of them have enjoyed great happiness and joy, also. Their experiences, like the whetstone brought to mind when girls are adolescents, have both sharpened and mellowed them. The sparks they flashed every now and then during our conversations were beautiful and enlightening.

The more time I spent with women this age, the more I wanted to see if, in fact, history reflects any meaningful accomplishments of women in their 60s. What I found just underscores my feelings of awe and encouragement.

For instance, did you know that Katharine Hepburn, at age sixty, won an Oscar for Best Actress in "Guess Who's Coming to Dinner?"

Margaret Thatcher (born in 1925, the same year as my mother), at age sixty and in her sixth year as England's Prime Minister, signed the historic Anglo-

Irish agreement aimed at resolving the Northern Ireland quandary.

Sixty was a busy age for Martha Stewart, as well. At that age, she sold 3,928 shares of ImClone stock and was jailed for insider trading (how dare a woman tread on traditionally male territory!). Even so, she was featured that same year in the PBS special "Martha Stewart in the Holiday Spirit" and published "Halloween: The Best of Martha Stewart Living." She is, after all, the consummate multi-tasker.

A sixty-year-old Mother Theresa received the John XXIII Peace Prize from Pope Paul VI.

Coretta Scott King, at sixty, organized "Mobilization Against Fear and Intimidation," a movement that carried on her late husband's great vision with her added passion and grace.

And the inimitable Gloria Steinem, at age sixty, wrote the book "Moving Beyond Words," in which she celebrates becoming, in her own words, a "nothing-to-lose older woman."

Who wouldn't aspire to these lofty marks of greatness at age thirty, much less at sixty? These women, and many others, took the tools forged by age, experience and wisdom and built something great, something to be recognized. And when you stop and think about it, don't we all? Your "something great" may be a close family with a solid foundation. It may be a career that took you places you'd never dreamed of going. It may be your contribution to helping those in need, or being a magnificent wife and lover, or becoming an academic scholar, or doing anything that matters to you and doing it well. We each define our own legacies.

More than a year ago, when I began writing this book, I had the opportunity to spend a month in a friend's divine beachfront home. I took this opportunity in the month of January, a time that, at the beach here in the South, is considered off-season. I looked forward to the quiet seclusion and sheer beauty of a beach not trampled and buzzing with tourists. To me, there's not much on this earth that's more calming and awe-inspiring.

What I didn't foresee was the golden opportunity to meet and talk with so many older couples who feel the same way about the beach in the off-season. "Snow birds," I believe these people are often called. These couples, the women especially, have had a great hand in building this book with me, and what an honor to be given access to such a wealth of life experience as these women allowed me.

There are many things I remember from that trip, treasures I took away and have stored safely in the lockbox of my own heart and mind – visual snapshots and priceless conversations I wouldn't trade for the world. But there was one particular event – it happened in a matter of just a few seconds – that I think sums up what we all wish for at the end of the day, whether we admit it or not. One evening, I had decided to venture out to a little hole-in-the-wall seafood place that was within walking distance of where I was staying. That's one of the thousands of hangups I have overcome in recent years; I have learned that a woman can walk into a restaurant, sit down and have a meal all by herself, and it's O.K. Anyway, I'm getting sidetracked here.

The approach to this little restaurant was a long boardwalk that stretched over the beach, and at that time of day, if you look to the right, you can see a spectacular sunset as the ocean opens its arms to envelop the shimmering sun. The view was so spectacular that I paused, leaned against the rail, and just stood still to enjoy the show until it was over. While I was engulfed in the quiet show and watching the sun set, I heard faint shuffling and soft whispers behind me. There were a few other people coming and going across the boardwalk, but these sounds were different enough to make me turn around and look. I will never forget what I saw.

An elderly couple, who looked to be in their mid- to late sixties, was walking arm in arm across the worn planks, he tall and strong and stable; she smaller, shakier and obviously stricken with an illness that hampered her ability to walk and speak. The whispering was her strong husband telling her to look to her left, so that she could take in the breathtaking show that God was so kindly offering beachgoers and diners that evening. The shuffling sound was the wife's halting gait as she felt for footing and used her cane in one hand, her husband's arm in the other. The couple stopped, she taking in the sunset and smiling, and he lovingly taking in the sun and the smile on his wife's face — and smiling himself. The woman's husband had obviously painstakingly taken the time to dress his wife for dinner, carefully applying her makeup and choosing just the right jewelry to go with her clothing. I will never forget that stolen snapshot tucked away in my head, or at least I hope I never do.

I remember thinking, as I took in all these things I've described for you here in a split second, that I was looking at a couple of great wealth. I have no idea what their financial situation might have been, but I was looking at bottomless wealth, riches beyond measure. I was looking at true love, and it made tears well up in my eyes when I witnessed it just as they are tearing now, as I'm retelling the story. At the end of the day, as we walk into our own sunset, what will we value? What will we hold dear? Whose beating heart will we hold so gently in our own hands?

That one voyeuristic moment I stole there on that boardwalk is all I want, all I will ever want because without it, does anything else matter? Maybe British playwright Arthur Pinero said it better than I could hope to here:

"Those who love deeply never grow old; they may die of old age, but they die young."

No, love is not an emotion or a fleeting desire or a mere attraction; it's taking the time to lovingly dress your wife in her favorite blouse and pearls because she can't do it herself. It's learning how to apply makeup to her face, so beautiful to you already, because you know it always mattered to her, and she'd want you to do it. It's making sure she sees the glorious sunset above and not just the careful placement of one foot in front of another so as not to stumble. It's leaning into your husband, feeling his strength and hearing his whispers meant only for you.

I don't believe it's weakness to desire and seek out true love. I don't believe it demonstrates weakness to lean on it and let it lean on us as needed throughout our lives; rather, I think it demonstrates the strength to surrender, the devotion to put someone else before oneself, and I believe that we only learn to do that, to live that, with age.

A woman in her sixties is very likely a strong creature, indeed. She's weathered; she's wise, and she's formidable:

"Time and trouble will tame an advanced young woman, but an advanced old woman is uncontrollable by any earthly force."
- Dorothy Sayers
(British crime writer and poet)

In other words, when a woman is equipped with self confidence and experience (both of which come with age), there's no stopping her when she puts her mind to something. Life is far from over at age sixty; in fact, many women tell me that it was right around that age when they really began to understand how to live life, with the right balance of "me" and "others" in it. Does luck, or being in the right place at the right time, have anything to do with eventual success? Sure it does, sometimes, but those occurrences without confidence and experience inevitably fizzle out to mean nothing.

The very little bit of advice I heard my mother utter with respect to women and aging had to do with, yes, grooming and appearance. For instance, my mother thought it was so unbecoming for an older woman to wear her hair long. I have no idea where she picked up that idea, but she did, all the same. Of course, when you hear your mother say something, you naturally assume for many years that she's right. Now, however, I think women my age and older who wear their hair long can look very elegant. But again, is it really the appearance of the woman that matters most, or what's inside her, what she offers, what she possesses? At sixty, we finally get that beauty is truly an inside job. Our eyes sparkle when we behold beauty, and that beauty can come in the form of a painting, a grandchild or a novel finished because it mattered to us. A life well lived is the best makeup on the market.

As I was tunneling through books and websites looking for achievements of women in their sixties and older, I found myself wondering whether they too were schooled as we were, having been given marriage, grooming and underwear advice with which to tackle life. The answer, I feel sure, is "of course they were." In fact, their life advice was probably even less inclusive than the majority of ours was.

One saying, which many of us have heard through the years and which is brought home again and again in the sixth decade of a person's life, is that "funerals come in three's." You see, it's been said that if we can get through our fifties without a heart attack squeezing the life out of us, and through our sixties without cancer reaching out from under the bed and wrapping its thin fingers around our ankles, then we're likely to live a very long life indeed.

Oddly enough, funerals do seem to come in three's. Look at the celebrity deaths of Michael Jackson, Farrah Fawcett and Ed McMahon in the summer of 2009. Three celebrities, three deaths in close proximity to one another. Is it really true, do you think, that funerals (or bad things in general) come in threes?

As strange as it sounds, I asked several of the "snow birds" I met at the beach last year that same question. After all, who would know better than elderly people about life's patterns and quirky trends? The general concensus among this population is that, if you wait long enough, you can predict pretty much anything coming in threes. Funerals, weddings, indigestion, family squabbles, bunions, you name it. Several of these people went further to say that the "funerals come in threes" wisdom is simply our very human way of putting a "cap" on our biggest fear — that of dying. It's a way of reducing that huge, unmanageable fear down to a flippant saying or a trend. I don't know what the truth of the matter is, but I can say this: Almost without fail, every elederly person with whom I spoke expressed faith, a belief in God, a belief that there is something out there that is bigger, stronger and infinitely wiser than we are.

Let's face it. By the time we reach sixty, if we haven't learned that we are in control of very little in our lives, we haven't learned a whole lot. If we haven't learned that there is a God, and we aren't Him, then we haven't been paying attention. There's something very comforting about knowing that we have an eternal "Big Brother," so to speak, who always sees the big picture and who always has our backs. There's comfort in knowing that we are not, in fact, responsible for and in control of everything around us. There's comfort in believing that there is a great design and that we are part of it, put in place with specific intent. Yes, faith (in my experience and research, anyway) is much more prevalent in older people than in young, bullet-proof, invincible people. Funny how that works.

Very often, it's that same faith that sees us through the dreaded news of poor health, through the burial of a husband or, God forbid, even that of a child. It's faith that gives us strength to watch our children struggle in their own lives, whether with addiction, divorce, or some other situation that could utterly and completely derail their precious lives. It's faith and experience that tell us when to sit silently by and when to step in.

After having spoken with so many women this age, I saw that the happiest were those who kept in regular communication with their children and those who had someone in their lives with which to share the days. The most peaceful and content were those who had a firm trust in God. Take that for what it's worth.

There are plenty of adventures still left to be unearthed at sixty, plenty of last-minute trips and exciting escapades left in us. We may saddle up a bit slower than we used to; we may take a few more breaks throughout our days, but the journey is very well worth continuing. It might even be a little more enjoyable because we savor its sweetness a little more, don't we? Yes, I think that's one of the wonderful things I've discovered now that I'm in my fifties, and from what I can tell, it only gets better: When we enjoy something, we enjoy it thoroughly and completely. The tangy juiciness in the first bite of a peach is not lost on us. A beautiful drive in the country always turns up one more thing we missed when we made the same drive last year. Musical notes seem clearer and more distinct (as do the lines on our faces), and they make the entire masterpiece even more breathtakingly moving (as do the lines on our faces).

Perhaps now more than ever before, we truly seize and live each day, because we understand on a very basic level that day's intrinsic, never-to-be-regained value.

BEING A WISE AND BEAUTIFUL WORK OF ART (OUR SEVENTIES AND BEYOND)

"Beautiful young people are accidents of nature, but beautiful old people are works of art."
- Eleanor Roosevelt
(First Lady of the United States from 1933 to 1945, wife of Franklin D. Roosevelt)

"You only live once, but if you do it right, once is enough."
- Mae West

Being a Wise and Beautiful Work of Art
(Our Seventies and Beyond)

I believe I mentioned near the very beginning of this book that I had the honor of interviewing a woman who was 88 years old at the time of our meeting. I also had the pleasure of sharing time and conversation with several woman in their 70s, and I can say honestly that I walked away from each of them a wiser, better woman for having spent that time. A woman who has reached these years has almost surely experienced wrenching heartache, soaring joy, disappointment, hope, accomplishment and pain. Just as a plain and unremarkable piece of coal undergoes tremendous changes at the very basest level (the rearrangement of atoms, I believe, is how it was explained to me), so does a woman who has travelled the long road from naïve youth to a wise and knowing age. A woman in this phase of her life is a book of secrets, softly bound and begging to be discovered and read by some fortunate soul. All that one has to do is set aside the time, get comfortable, and ask that her secrets be revealed.

"Frances Mathilda Amhurst Bowen," the wrinkled, beautiful, well-spoken woman answered me when I asked for her full name. Hers is the only actual full name I've used in this book, because she insisted that I do so and frankly, she spoke it so pointedly and clearly when I asked that there was really no other choice. Frances dressed to perfection for our interview and even had her hair done just the day before (a fact which she pointed out to me several times, but I suspect she's had that standing appointment since the mid-1970s or so). She wore a pink linen suit and, though she walks with the aid of a walker, stood and pirouetted to show it off when I remarked about the color and style.

Up until about five years ago, Frances lived in her own home, the home in which she had raised her six children, by herself. Her husband passed away in the late 1990s, and though she lives in an upscale and very comfortable retirement home, Frances is not very happy about her current circumstances (a theme I found repeated quite often when interviewing women in this age bracket who had been uprooted from their homes). She is proud and very sharp, and before I knew it, I found myself answering her questions rather than the other way around. Frances is a delightful woman, but it took me a few minutes not to feel, well, intimidated in her presence. She questioned whether I had dressed the way I had that day for comfort or perhaps for a long trip, or do I always dress like that (I was wearing my customary leggings and loose top – my husband calls it my uniform)? She asked me how many children I have. When I answered "four – two from my husband's first marriage and two from mine," she gave me a look that skillfully combined shock, disdain and pity all in the same expression. Shock, because of the broken marriage situation and pity, I'm assuming, stemming from the fact that I only had a paltry four children to her six.

For a little more than three hours, Frances and I sipped tea and let the conversation wander wherever it would, with me only redirecting it a time or two. This little woman, who by now has, God willing, celebrated her 90th birthday, took me back to her girlhood days with memories that could have been plucked from yesterday, they were relayed with such sharp clarity. She had to struggle a bit when we'd touch on events from the past ten years or so, but I've been told by my father's own neurologist that this phenomenon is not uncommon in an aging mind. Short-term memory, for some reason, fades with age, but long-term memory sets up housekeeping and stays a while in the healthy mind of an elderly person.

Frances raised six children – in her own words – by herself. Her husband had been a banker and had travelled quite a bit, but she hinted to me more than once that she suspected his "travel" had been more pleasure than business.

This woman's frankness surprised me; I'm not sure what I expected before I actually had my audience with her. I'm embarrassed to say that I think I expected an addled, fragile little woman who would be more proper than honest, an interview with an 88-year-old woman that would give this book necessary balance and a sweet touch. What I got was a delightfully blunt, sharp, funny, clever woman who believe me, was doing me the favor rather than I her by giving me a few hours of her time.

Yes, Frances told me, she and her family had been blessed financially, especially considering the bleak financial climate that was the backdrop for much of her life as a young woman. She was also quick to tell me that her husband had been unfaithful to her almost from day one of their marriage, but a divorce would have simply been out of the question. "He loved us in his own way," she told me, looking past the few other residents who had wandered into the room we were using, past them and out the window that overlooked one of many well-manicured gardens. "I would never have left him. The scandal it would have brought our families! And what would I do with all those children and no husband?" That last question indicated to me that she had at least considered the possibility of leaving, but the mechanics of such a choice were simply not in place for women at that time. In truth, I'm not so sure they're in place for women now, are they? It's a tough choice with tough consequences even in today's "enlightened" society. But even Frances' acknowledgement to me, a complete stranger, that her husband had been unfaithful to her during their entire marriage was not enough to dampen her spirits. She leaned over and slyly whispered to me that his meanderings were at times a blessing, freeing up her time to do as she pleased while other women attended to his "needs" (as she called them). I couldn't help myself, and I asked her whether she had ever strayed outside the boundaries of her marriage, especially since her husband had been so openly unfaithful. She leaned back in her chair and thought for a minute before answering my (probably rude and impertinent) question. "Why would I have done that? I was not brought up that way and besides, do you really think I had the time for such nonsense? I had a family." Funny but not surprising, I suppose, that she had a family that kept her from straying, but her husband did not see things the same way. It's amazing what kind of light perspective sheds on one's life circumstances, isn't it?

This sweet, elegant lady also shared with me that she had actually given birth to eight children in her lifetime, but one of them had died at birth and the other when the little boy was less than a year old. Of all the stories she pulled from memory that afternoon, that one etched the deepest lines of pain across her sweet face. My heart broke for her as she spoke; she told the story as though it had just happened yesterday, not more than fifty years ago. I suppose the pain never really dulls. I hope I never have to find out.

Frances and I wandered leisurely through topics that included work (she worked outside their home briefly when her husband "disappeared" for nearly a year, away on "business," leaving her to fend for herself and her children), childbirth (thank God for advances in medical science), her siblings (all of whom by then had passed away), education (she is one of a relative few from that era who earned a four-year degree), economics, "binding unmentionables" (girdles and such) and of course, her own mother. I walked away from that interview much richer than I had arrived.

Every 70-plus age woman with whom I spent time over the past year or so has surprised (and impressed) me with their open honesty. I really expected these older women to be more hush-hush about certain topics: sex, marriage and their limited choices, to name a few. I was hilariously wrong. Sometimes, they had to wait for me to catch up with the conversation before continuing.

In fact, the most-talked-about topics among these women (at least with me) were sex and marriage, believe it or not. I sensed among these women that they liked sex, they enjoyed their sexuality and understood its power – always had – but that they felt supremely bound by the Western confines placed upon it. Of course they didn't use the term "Western confines," but it's here on this side of the planet that we treat sex with such taboo on one hand, and exploit it with such reckless abandon on the other. "It's confusing!" as one woman told me. Even at age 74, I could hear the frustration in her voice.

Being a Wise and Beautiful Work of Art
(Our Seventies and Beyond)

I'm going to share something with you that I hope is O.K. I'm not mentioning any names, so I'm not betraying any confidences, but women in this age group tell me in one way or another that they actually feel more free to enjoy a life of intimacy now than they did forty years ago. Is it because they can finally put S-E-X into perspective? Is it because they finally understand that they don't have to care what everyone else thinks about their personal lives? Is it because they hear for so many years that "nice girls don't do 'it,'" but "it" was pretty important for many, many years, to both women and to men? That, I can't answer accurately. Maybe I can in twenty years or so, but I can't now. I can only draw an educated conclusion: These women have seen many things throughout their lives. They have married and had sex (not always in that order, but for the record that's the order that I'll use). They have made babies, raised them and said "goodbye" to them, one way or another. They have married and often said "goodbye" to that person, too. In other words, the things that mattered, the things that raised eyebrows, so many years ago aren't quite as important as society told us they were. The things that matter are the people, the experiences, the living of a life, not what other people think about how that life's been lived. What a silly thing to worry about, we've come to learn, when it comes to what other people may think of us. It's like worrying about red lipstick and clean underwear.

MaryLee, 78 years old, is the woman who clued me in to the educated guess I just made. At age 36, MaryLee – a mother of two young children at the time and wife of a prominent doctor in her Southern home town – had an affair with a man, who was also married at the time. The affair was short lived and never uncovered by either duped spouse, but it never faded from MaryLee's memory. The whispers and secret accusations spread throughout her hometown, as they will in small towns, and she lived in fear for years that her husband would learn the truth. She carried the shame that she felt with her for more than forty years, and the sting never faded. Even so, she managed to raise those two children, and an eventual third, to be happy, productive adults. She made a comfortable, warm home, and she buried her husband not two years before she sat across a table from me and my trusty notepad and talked with me for the purpose of writing this book. She told me without hesitation that she loved her husband dearly. Yet, she had always felt less, felt diminished, by the choice she made that forever changed her life inside her head and her heart.

"It wasn't until I asked our pastor what to do, how to lighten this burden in my heart, that I learned to live with what I had done. He told me that I needed to seek forgiveness from my Father in Heaven, and I did." According to MaryLee, her heart was lighter from that moment on. With respect to whether to tell her husband, well, the pastor left that decision up to her. He did warn her against unloading her burden just to make herself feel better, when it could very well destroy her husband, their marriage and family. She made up her mind to never tell him about the affair, ever. And she never did.

She also shared with me that, while her husband was dying, he forgave her for her indiscretion, however brief but hurtful it was. He had known all along, but he loved her enough to carry on with their lives as though it had never happened. "I don't think it was until right then, before he died, that I knew how much I really loved him," MaryLee told me. Her pooling tears made her crystal-blue eyes even bluer.

I have reviewed my notes from that interview dozens of times, and her words bring tears to my own eyes every single time I read them. How much time do we waste in this lifetime worrying about what other people think, trying to impress others? How much time do we throw away on guilt? Each of these women taught me a little bit more, enough to draw this conclusion: It's not about what the crowd may think that matters; it's about what the people who matter think. MaryLee might just be the first to tell you that.

Well, on to another matter that arises and must be dealt with very often in our seventies. I'd say the majority of women I interviewed in this age bracket were either living with one of their children or in a retirement community. Most of them seemed to have made the transition all right, but not a single one of them could tell me that they felt at home in someone else's abode. They could all tell me that they were being treated well, and they even had to admit that they felt safer living with other people than they did living alone. Still, they missed their homes and everything that went with living in them.

Something else I noticed and found very interesting was that, with the exception of only two of these women, they each had a cat or a dog. They had something to care for, something that needed them. I don't think that's a coincidence. In fact, I think being needed and loved goes a long way toward enriching and even prolonging life. As women, we are used to being caregivers, to being needed. It's part of what makes us tick. Having a pet around who loves us unconditionally and who depends on us for its well-being is therapeutic, the ultimate win-win.

Here's something else I found hilarious when talking with women who lived in retirement communities or assisted living communities. You see, in that age bracket (seventies, eighties and even higher), women definitely comprise the majority of the population. Men are in short supply (my dad will be the first to tell you that). Some women couldn't care less about the men-to-women ratio where they live, but then there are others who revert right back to those adolescent and teen behaviors, so second-nature to a female: scouting, competing, gossiping and competing some more, for the ultimate prize of getting the guy. I mean really, isn't there something poetic and just outright funny about that? Even after all they've learned about men, all they've learned about what they are and what they aren't, the man is still the prize, and all's fair in love and war.

I know what I've witnessed where my dad lives. When he first moved in to the retirement community, women who already lived there had gotten wind of the new man moving in well before the move-in date. They began bringing him cookies and homemade meals, inviting him to social events, doing all the things they know attracts most men. When one would arrive with a plate of cookies and another was leaving after having brought Dad some homemade stew, the thinly-veiled catty remarks and insinuations would begin.

"I'd tell your father to be careful around that one. She's already had four husbands."

"Be careful what you say around her; she's a busy-body." And with smiles and girlish flirtation in their voices, they would turn to my dad, "Dave," and present their offerings, smiling and swishing on the way out.

It's just second-nature, isn't it?

THE LIFETIME OF A WOMAN

It bears repeating:

"The woman I was yesterday, introduced me to the woman I am today, which makes me very excited about meeting the woman I will become tomorrow."

This one quote, this single short sentence, illustrates the essence of what it is to be a woman. From the moment we arrive screaming and protesting into the bright lights and chilly air of this world, we begin to change. For many years, we change to accommodate what others expect of us, to reflect what they want to see. We feel an innate need to be all things to all people, to make the lives of those we love good, comfortable, warm and safe. It's only natural for a woman to feel that need, for as we concluded earlier, we are nurturers by nature.

Through this process of fluid evolution, we ebb to serve our families; we flow to discover ourselves. We derive unparalleled satisfaction from seeing our children be happy and successful – however they define both of those conditions. When we eventually come to the realization that we, too, deserve happiness and satisfaction, and yes even "fulfillment," (I usually detest that word when as it applies to the evolution of women, but here, it fits), we build up the courage to go get all of those things. When we realize that we too deserve, hopefully we're healthy enough to do something about it.

I have come to the conclusion that something I've suspected for many years is actually true: A woman's real beauty, her pheromonal attraction, is derived from the words written in her own book, the book that details her life, verbatim. Conversely, if a woman has lived a hard and bitter life, her appearance, her presence, takes on that same aura. Here's something else I've concluded though, and some of you may disagree, but I feel confident in asserting this opinion because it's been my pleasure to observe over this year and with these women:

No matter the circumstances of a woman's life, whether she's endured pain, loss or abuse, there is a dewy, untouched bud at her center that awakens to kindness, love, respect and acknowledgement. Yes, she will curve to fit her life's circumstances and those of her loved ones. But when those she loves occasionally curve to fit her life, to fit her needs, her heart wells. The young girl at the center of her being is awakened and renewed. Her countenance changes. Lines are smoothed. Eyes are clear and open. And beauty does indeed become an inside job.

Young women have to slog through so much just to uncover themselves, and some women, sadly, never do. Some women never learn to see past what others think of them, which is a true tragedy, because without that ability we can never know who we really are. Too often, all a woman sees is her reflection in her boyfriend(s) eyes or in her husband's, or in her parents', or perhaps in her children's. She misses the true beauty of who she really is, because reflections are never completely accurate, always just a bit skewed.

It's been said that our ability to be good mothers improves with every generation. Following that theory, I am a better mother than my mother was, and my daughter will be a better mother than I was. I hope to God that theory is accurate, because I know my mother fell short of perfect and so have I. So will my daughter, I suspect, but I already see that she'll be a terrific mom. She's kind and compassionate, conscientious and just, well, good. She has a very strong sense of who she is, too, a sense that took me more than half my lifetime to develop. She will pass on lessons and axioms, advice and examples, to her daughter. More importantly, she'll instill that sense of self in all of her children, because she has had it herself for a long while. It will be difficult, especially during those agonizing teen years, but she will do it.

Womanhood is a condition to be celebrated, monthly reminders and all. We are the wellsprings of life. We are comfort. We are beauty, defined in thousands of little ways. We are gifted with something some call "intuition," which is in reality an amped-up ability to feel, to empathize, to just know. We are magical creatures, so easily bruised, yet so easily uplifted. If you're a woman, celebrate that blessing. If you're a man, celebrate the women in your life, because as wonderful as they are today, they'll be even better in a year or two, or ten or twenty.

We may likely never be seen as being equal to men, but is that such a bad thing? I love men – absolutely adore them (my husband and son occupy the top of that list) – but why set the bar lower than it should be, ladies? Men have gifts, and so do we.

Maybe I'm biased, but I think we may have the advantage.

"A girl should be two things: classy and fabulous."
Coco Chanel
(haute couture designer)

About the author

Carole Townsend is a wife, mom, newspaper reporter and blogger living in suburban Atlanta. Formerly a Fortune 500 Marketing Executive, she always loved to write and to tell stories, putting her own particular spin on them. When her youngest child moved away to go to college, she seized the opportunity to pursue her desire to weave words into books and spice them up with humor as only she can do.

She and her husband Marc now live at home with their three rescue dogs – two Golden Retrievers and a Chihuahua.